APL

— ACCREDITATION OF PRIOR LEARNING —

A PRACTICAL
GUIDE FOR
PROFESSIONALS

APL

ACCREDITATION OF PRIOR LEARNING

A PRACTICAL GUIDE FOR PROFESSIONALS

Susan Simosko

KOGAN
PAGE

First published in 1991
Reprinted in 1992

Kogan Page Limited
120 Pentonville Road
London N1 9JN

British Library Cataloguing in Publication Data
A CIP record for this book is available from the British Library.

ISBN 0 7494 0474 4

Typeset by DP Photosetting, Aylesbury, Bucks
Printed and bound by Clays Ltd, St. Ives PLC

Contents

Acknowledgements

Writing a book is never an easy task, even under ideal conditions. And this book was written under far less than desirable conditions. So it is with sincerest thanks that I would like to acknowledge the invaluable professional help given to me by Jonathan Stewart who provided major research and editorial assistance and an easy manner that belied the stress under which we all worked; by Cathy Cook who filled in more than one gap for me in meeting other contractual obligations and who always seemed to offer the right suggestion at the right time; by Gloria Savage who offered not only support, encouragement and serenity but a willingness to divert phone calls on a regular basis; Christine Cookson who made sure all our bills got paid; and Anita Currie who joined us somewhere mid-book and helped each of us in a variety of ways.

Lastly, I would like to thank my husband, Graham Debling, for his thoughtful questions, creative ideas, loving encouragement and more than one Saturday evening spent reading drafts.

Susan Simosko
May 1991

Chapter 1

APL: What's it all about?

Introduction

All over the world the drive is on to make better use of existing resources. Nowhere is this more true than in the area of human resource development. Educators, trainers, employers and government policy makers, regardless of nation, seem to be saying much the same thing: that as nations we must put individuals first and 'provide opportunities whereby everyone can make maximum use of their potential' (CBI, 1989).

Educators and trainers, often pressed to do more with less, worry that they are wasting too much time teaching people things they already know and can do. Growing numbers of employers express concern that individual employees are becoming demotivated, unwilling or unable to respond to future demands and changes within an industry. And government policy makers continue to grapple with the need to effectively foster positive change in organisations, industry and individuals to ensure a viable economic future and a stable, equitable social climate for all.

Clearly in each context there are a number of ways these problems are being addressed, nationally, regionally and locally. One important way that is challenging many long-established ideas about education and training is through the introduction of a process called the recognition or accreditation of prior learning (APL). In Britain, Australia, North America and elsewhere, professionals are introducing APL in an effort to motivate individuals, make more effective use of training resources, increase the flexibility of organisations, and cultivate attitudes that value life-long learning. In so doing, those who introduce and deliver APL services are also enhancing their own professional development as they acquire new skills and work in new environments with increasingly diverse groups of people.

APL: what is it?

The terminology

First, a word about the terms used to describe the process: in the USA, where much of the early work originated, the process is usually called 'prior learning assessment (PLA)'; in Australia, where the concept is just taking hold, the term most often used is the 'recognition of prior learning (RPL)'; and in the UK the words include not only 'accreditation of prior learning (APL)' but also 'accreditation of prior achievement (APA)' and 'assessment of prior experiential learning (APEL)'. A lot of energy has gone into getting the words right within each nation and context, but the basic concept remains the same: that through a systematic and valid assessment process, an individual's skills and knowledge can be formally recognised and credited, regardless of how, when or why they were obtained.

One thing APL surely is not: credit for life experience. People do not receive recognition or credit for what they experience in life. Although all that a person learns in life may be of value to that individual, in the APL process, it is the attainments, skills and knowledge, or competences* – all of which may have been attained experientially – that are recognised and credited. Although the basic concept seems clear enough, inappropriate terminology has led to many misunderstandings and a belief in some people that the process is a 'soft option' towards obtaining

---

* Competences is a term which has been developed in Britain to refer to skills, knowledge and abilities. Other countries may use the word 'competencies'.

qualifications. Those who have been through the process or those professionals who have committed themselves to setting up a sound programme will know otherwise!

Much concern about the term APL has focused on the notion of 'prior', for in truth all human learning and achievements occur in the past – whether acquired ten years, ten days, or ten minutes ago. The original introduction of the word 'prior', however, was intended to emphasise that what was being assessed was outside – independent of – any particular *current* formal academic course. The increasingly blurred lines between 'training' and 'education' have put a strain on the word, for indeed, many people identify learning they obtain from on-going employer-based training programmes or non-credit adult education courses, for example, as they begin to identify their 'prior learning'.

The words themselves are not critical to the process, although indeed great efforts are being made around the world, in many different languages, to modify the term to more accurately reflect the process.

The concept

Most simply, the accreditation of prior learning is a process that enables people of all ages, backgrounds and attitudes to receive formal recognition for skills and knowledge they already possess. It is built on the premise that people can and do learn throughout their entire lives and that much of this informal and uncertificated learning can be equated with the skills and knowledge expected of learners completing more traditional and formal learning programmes.

The type of recognition people receive varies with the context: sometimes it is in the form of credit towards a particular vocational or academic qualification; sometimes it is in the form of exemption from some portion of an educational or training programme; and almost always it is used as a development tool by both the individual undergoing the process and the educational or training providers offering the service.

Intrinsic to the concept of APL is the notion that people can be assessed without regard for any particular learning or training programme. As part of the APL process, the focus is on *what* an individual has learned, not the time, place, or method of learning, or even the motivation of the learner.

Essentially APL is about four basic processes:

- *identifying* what an individual knows and can do;
- *equating* those skills and knowledge with specific standards, course or qualification requirements;
- *assessing* the individual against those standards or requirements; and
- *crediting* the learner in the appropriate manner.

It is the systematic approach to each of these that ensures a sound and equitable APL programme.

APL: who benefits?

Research over the past 20 years has provided significant evidence of the benefits of APL to both individuals and organisations. Individuals benefit in a variety of ways from the APL process. Specifically, as an outcome of the recognition of what has been learnt, it enables them to:

1. build on their experiences and not have to relearn what they already know and can do;
2. shorten the time required to complete formal qualifications;
3. focus on their own development and training needs;
4. recognise the value of their accomplishments; and
5. often save significant sums of money.

Significantly, APL also appears to serve as a powerful motivator for individuals to seek new learning opportunities and complete recognised qualifications. Both in the UK and the USA there is growing evidence that adults completing the process grow more self-confident, are willing to take greater responsibility for their own development and have changed – generally more positive – attitudes about educational and training organisations. Even for those who already have a strong sense of self-confidence, the process seems to lead to more focused learning and increased self-awareness.

In quite a different vein, APL helps people to earn needed qualifications more expediently. These qualifications, whether they be National Vocational Qualifications (NVQs) in Britain or associate diplomas in Australia or degrees in the USA, often enable people to re-enter the job market, explore new career paths, or seek promotions within their existing organisations. In each case, the qualification represents a valuable tool for empowering individuals and enabling them to move more readily in their chosen directions – directions which often mean that more effective use is made of the individual's skills and knowledge, leading to greater job and personal satisfaction.

Organisations also gain from the introduction of APL. They find they can:

1. maximise the effective use of their educational and training resources;
2. better meet the needs of individual clients, students or employees;
3. motivate their clients or employees to participate more willingly in, and to complete, the programmes;
4. provide equal opportunities to a greater range of clients; and
5. integrate APL with ongoing services or programmes.

APL and its constituent steps can be used by an organisation for any number of purposes, for example, as a diagnostic tool to identify an individual's strengths and weaknesses. To be fully effective APL needs to be associated with learner-centered training or educational programmes. APL and such programmes lead to more effective use of resources. When APL is used by colleges and universities, the institution often sees more highly motivated students who are eager to complete the certificate, diploma or degree programmes on which they enrol.

Who are the learners?

Learners in the APL framework include anyone who needs, wants or could benefit by receiving recognition or qualifications for his/her learning. The following examples of Jim, Sharon, Amina and Charles illustrate the diversity of backgrounds learners bring with them to APL.

JIM

Jim is 35, married and has two children. He has worked for seven years as a computer salesman. He also has worked his way through an open-learning pack in selling and has participated in three on-the-job training workshops on presentation, negotiation and time-management skills.

Jim is also a member of the local Junior Chamber of Commerce, where he takes a lead in organising Chamber functions and events. He enjoys this challenge, which often involves his delegating tasks to his colleagues and managing a limited budget.

In Jim's current organisation internally advertised positions for managers often arise in various areas. Jim wants to move into one of these management positions; however, he realises that without any formal management qualification, he would be unlikely to get as far as the first interview. Jim knows that he has the experience necessary for the job, but just needs the opportunity to prove it. APL will allow Jim to gain credit towards a management qualification, which in turn will enable him to qualify for a job interview.

SHARON

Sharon left school after obtaining three A-levels in chemistry, physics and biology. She was always interested in chemistry and had obtained the necessary grades to embark on a degree in the subject. However, after leaving school she accepted a job as a technician in a chemistry laboratory at a nearby university. She has been working in this position for over four years.

Sharon's job as a technician is much wider than just preparing equipment and experiments. She has also been involved in giving demonstrations to undergraduates on liquid crystal displays and has read widely around the topic, which she finds fascinating. She has also been carrying out some research herself on liquid crystal displays, which she hopes to publish jointly with some of the research staff, who treat her as an equal and respect both her interest and enthusiasm for the field, neither of which is a necessary requirement of her job.

Often research staff with whom she works advertise for research assistants. Sharon now wants to move into research full-time and feels she has the necessary experience to take on one of these jobs. However, university admission procedures stipulate that a degree is necessary for research positions. Sharon does not want to leave her technician job to study for a three-year degree. Not only does she need the money, she wants to keep in touch with ongoing research. APL will enable Sharon to gain credit for a large part of the degree programme and obtain her degree in a time-shortened period while still retaining her current job.

AMINA

Amina is 29 years old and has been working as a cook in her father's speciality restaurant since leaving school. She has never had any formal training in catering, but has practically run her father's restaurant during recent years. She learned everything about catering from her father and from on-the-job experience.

The restaurant is very popular with locals and appears in a number of good food guides. Unfortunately, Amina's father is getting old and is no longer interested in running the restaurant. Amina herself has enjoyed working in the restaurant but soon will be getting married and leaving her family home. Recently she has been applying for jobs in catering closer to where she intends to live. However, Amina has found that despite her experience, most modern restaurants require a catering qualification before hiring anyone. Obviously, Amina does not want, nor does she have the time, to go to college to relearn what she already knows. APL would enable Amina to acquire a catering qualification and therefore allow her career to progress much more quickly.

CHARLES

Charles is 31 and single. Immediately after finishing school with few qualifications, he joined the navy. He spent five years in the service where he had the opportunity to visit many fascinating places throughout the world. Often, on shore-leave he would make a point of visiting places off the beaten track and away from the commercial ports. He kept a diary of what he encountered on his travels, noting peculiar features of the landscape and customs of local inhabitants.

On board ship, Charles spent his spare time reading books and local literature on the places he had visited. When not reading, he would be writing his diary on his thoughts and perceptions. Through his time in the navy Charles learned a lot about cultural differences and the diversity of local customs and rituals.

After completing his time, Charles worked for short periods in various jobs, but found it hard to find one which matched the excitement of the navy. One Sunday, he read an advertisement in a newspaper for volunteers to embark on a three-month field trip in the African rainforests. The organisers of the trip were investigating the detrimental effects felling of the rainforests was having on the African tribes. Charles saw this as a great opportunity to regain his interest in different cultures and as a route out of a mundane job. He applied to be a volunteer and after a number of interviews was accepted. He enjoyed the field trip immensely, during which he developed a good rapport and working relationship with the research team. He did not go home after the three months but continued working in Africa for a number of months, until the research team's funds ran out.

On returning home Charles managed to get a non-professional job with the research team he had been working with in Africa. Although this job was not highly paid, it was ideal for Charles. It gave him access to topical research and information on tribes throughout Africa and was not a 9-to-5 job. From time to time, opportunities also arose for Charles to visit Africa and other countries with the team.

Charles has begun thinking about the possibilities of obtaining a degree, particularly as all his colleagues at work have one. He believes that obtaining a university degree in anthropology, while not essential for his career, would give him a deep sense of personal satisfaction and might enable him to gain a greater level of independence in his organisation. He would like to use APL to earn as much credit for his prior learning as possible.

As exemplified by these four people, adult learners identify many reasons for seeking recognition and credit for their prior learning. For each, however, it brings the promise of greater personal and/or professional satisfaction.

Where did APL come from?

The basic premise of APL – that people learn by doing – has been around for centuries. There are many deep traditions of experiential learning easily recognised, from the writings of many Greek philosophers right through to the work of later philosophers such as John Locke, John Stewart Mill and others. In the context of the twentieth century, thinkers such as Jean Piaget, John Dewey, Kurt Lewin and David Kolb have each stressed the critical importance of experiential learning to human growth and development.

It is also possible to analyse a number of social movements to understand the origins of APL. For example, during the Middle Ages, the guild system required that the master determine when an apprentice was ready to move on to journeyman status and the journeyman on to master status. To no small extent this was a type of assessment and accreditation of prior learning.

From quite a different point of view, medical students are required to serve a period of internship before becoming professional doctors. These internships provide the experiential learning opportunities that reading books and attending lectures cannot and are viewed as essential to the development of the competent doctor.

Similarly, classroom teachers the world over also provide experiential learning opportunities. It is difficult to imagine any biology, music or computer programing course not containing a laboratory or action-learning experience. The belief that experiential learning is intrinsic to the development of any competent biologist, musician or computer programer (to provide but a few examples) is unquestioned in our modern training and educational world.

So if we believe that experiential learning is so critical to human experience and so deeply embedded in many of our current traditions, what is so unique about APL? Simply answered, APL forces us to recognise that *any* experience, whether formal or informal (and maybe even accidental!), may provide a powerful learning opportunity for an individual and that with proper assessment, the outcomes of that learning experience can be formally recognised and credited.

The current APL movement developed in the USA during the late 1960s and 1970s. It was originally conceived as a research project at the Educational Testing Service in Princeton, New Jersey (CAEL, 1975). There were three basic questions to be investigated during the three-year study period:

1. Is it possible to equate non-college learning with that offered in traditional college curricula?
2. If it is possible, can assessment techniques other than paper-and-pencil tests be used to evaluate the outcomes of this learning?
3. If such a system proves feasible, would it be possible to integrate the ensuing model in current educational programmes?

This project, known as the Cooperative Assessment of Experiential Learning Project, involved ten colleges and universities. Outcomes of the project demonstrated that:

1. It was possible to equate non-college learning with that of traditional college curricula.
2. It was feasible to use a wide variety of evidence in conducting valid and reliable assessments.
3. The emerging process could well be embedded in existing educational programmes and was of particular use with adults who were entering for the first time or returning to college or university with rich and varied experiential learning.

Today more than 1200 colleges and universities in the USA offer assessment and accreditation of prior learning programmes with a growing number emerging in the UK, Canada and Australia. In addition, greater numbers of employers are becoming involved in the work, most often fostering APL through joint ventures with a wide range of educational or training providers. The Council for Adult and Experiential Learning (CAEL), a leading national organisation in the USA, is actively engaged in promoting these joint ventures to bring APL and other educational and training programmes to people in the work place.

The development of APL in Britain

The assessment of prior experiential learning (APEL) was introduced in Britain in the 1980s largely as an outgrowth of on-going work in the USA. In 1980 the US-based Kellogg Foundation offered CAEL $25,000 (Gamson, 1989) to develop a British/American Scholars Exchange Programme. Through this programme a wide range of UK educators and policy makers visited American institutions that were advocating or implementing APL. Under the leadership of Norman Evans, now director of the Learning from Experience Trust, a number

19

of APEL projects were developed, primarily in higher education and most often for purposes of access to higher education by adults. Unlike the work that followed in the latter half of the 1980s, these early projects were not based on standards of competence or even learning outcomes. Rather they used profiling systems that provided evidence of both the need for such a service and a useful methodology that could be applied in a variety of higher education contexts.

This early APEL work coincided with a number of other developments, namely the government's call for a more flexible, adaptable workforce; training programmes that were more responsive to the needs of employers *and* individuals; greater access to education and training for greater numbers of people, and so forth.

As far back as 1981 the Manpower Services Commission (MSC)* published a far-sighted review of vocational education and training in the UK called *A New Training Initiative* (HMSO, 1981). This stated the problem in unequivocal terms and provided a mandate:

> Britain needs a flexible, adaptable work force to cope with the uncertainties which cloud the future. The technological revolution and the need to become more competitive present real challenges for as far ahead as we can see. Markets and prices for products, processes and services will continue to fluctuate. Firms and individuals must either adapt to change or become its victims.

Developments in Scotland also contributed to and provided a framework for offering APL. Growing out of a decade-long interest in criterion-referenced assessment, in 1983 the Scottish Education Department announced an intention to convert the

---

* While the MSC was a quasi-autonomous organisation, it was staffed by civil servants within the Employment Department. With the demise of the commission in 1988, the functions and staff were assimilated back into the Employment Department.

further education craft and technician education curriculum to a criterion-referenced format based on clear and explicit learning outcome statements. In implementing this Action Plan, as it was called, a decision was also taken to adopt a modular structure, replacing qualifications acquired by end-of-course examinations with a structure that typically replaced one year's curriculum with 20 modules.

At an early stage in the development, it was realised that if the desired learning was expressed in clear and explicit criterion-referenced learning outcome format, learners could be assessed against the expected outcomes as soon as it was apparent that they had met the standards. Achievement of credit would no longer be tied to a fixed period of study. Indeed it was now possible to be assessed against the learning outcomes without attending a single class. Scotland had essentially found its own way to APL.

The 1986 White Paper *Working Together – Education and Training* (DE, 1986) lay further groundwork for the introduction of APL: 'Qualifications and standards are not luxuries. They are necessities, central to securing a competent and adaptable workforce. Economic performance and individual job satisfaction both depend on maintaining and improving standards of competence'.

This same White Paper established the National Council for Vocational Qualifications (NCVQ) which was to take the lead in the reform of vocational qualifications which were to be based on nationally recognised standards of competence.

NCVQ also expressed a commitment to a unit-based structure. It came to the same conclusions regarding the potential of APL as had been reached in Scotland two years earlier. In 1987 the MSC (now the Employment Department) first mounted an exploratory study and then two major feasibility projects to investigate the potential of applying APL processes to National Vocational Qualifications (NVQs) and, in Scotland, National Certificate modules.

Outcomes of the feasibility studies

As a result of these major feasibility studies, NCVQ, Scottish Vocational Education Council (SCOTVEC) and a number of the major awarding bodies endorsed the concept of APL and established policies and recommended implementation procedures. These organisations, along with the participating further education colleges, have identified the key features of a sound APL service. These include:

1. A commitment by the organisation to establish a clear policy for the recognition, assessment and accreditation of prior learning.
2. A concrete plan to integrate APL with other educational and training services.
3. A strong commitment to staff development and on-going team building throughout the organisation.
4. Trained advisors and assessors.
5. A named person responsible for the management of the APL service.
6. A clear marketing strategy.
7. Modular instruction or access to alternative learning resources for all candidates.
8. A commitment to offer a range of assessment-on-demand services.

In addition, the feasibility studies provided the basis for a number of other projects, many funded by the Employment Department. Each was designed to investigate APL in different contexts and for different groups of people. It is worth noting a number of these projects to understand the full scale and impact APL is having on training and education in the UK. The 1990 Employment Department publication *Accreditation of Prior Learning: A Training Agency Perspective*, gives a full reference to these projects, (ED, 1990).

Occupational developments

Management

The Confederation of British Industry (CBI), the Foundation for Management Education (FME) and the British Institute of Management (BIM) with government support established a national organisation to:

1. develop a coherent Code of Practice to foster better training for managers;
2. develop national standards of competence for managers; and
3. promote the individual development of British managers.

This organisation is called the National Forum for Management Education and Development (NFMED). Its operational arm is the Management Charter Initiative (MCI) which is supported by a membership of more than 800 employers, representing 7.5 million employees, or about one quarter of the UK workforce.

As part of its work, the MCI learned that very few British managers over 35 years of age have had *any* formal management training or development. They also learned that most managers, regardless of age, do not *expect* to receive any management education or training. Although many managers do have some sort of formal qualifications, these are most often in professional areas such as accounting, engineering, chemistry, or at craft and technician level. Very few have qualifications reflecting what they do as managers (Tjok-a-Tam, 1991).

In conjunction with the development of national standards, a major APL project, supported by the Employment Department, was launched in 1989. It was designed to help managers:

1. recognise their strengths *and* weaknesses;
2. receive formal recognition towards national management qualifications; and
3. take greater responsibility for their own development and education as managers.

Working with a range of providers including further and higher education institutions, management development specialists (both schools and independent firms and associations), two large employers (British Gas and British Rail) and the BIM, more than 400 experienced managers completed the APL process in a nine-month period. Almost all earned credit towards a recognised management qualification; some were able to earn the full award.

As an outcome of the success of this project, APL is being integrated with all of MCI's on-going initiatives under the banner of 'Crediting Competence'. Managers throughout the UK are now able to have their skills and knowledge – competence – assessed and recognised in the form of credit towards national qualifications. Drawing from the initial project, MCI staff and membership are convinced that APL will serve as an essential development tool for individual managers and as a valuable training needs analysis tool for employers. Because the APL work is based on best-practice competence-based national standards, it is anticipated that greater numbers of managers will seek to meet the standards, obtain qualifications reflecting what they know and can do, and otherwise assume greater responsibility for their own training and development.

Other vocational areas
APL has also been implemented at a number of colleges of further education in a wide range of vocational disciplines. Candidates coming forward have been able to earn credit towards National Vocational Qualifications in areas as diverse as hotel and catering, computing, office procedures, business studies, and automotive technology. Although the actual numbers have been small (reflecting the same pattern as in North America), the impact of these various programmes has been highly significant.

The use of APL within these areas has served to motivate many competent people who previously had little or no regard for formal educational programmes to seek qualifications *and* new learning. It also has enabled people to value what they know and can do and, perhaps most importantly, it has demonstrated to individuals that they *have and can* learn. It is perhaps a sad commentary that so many intelligent, competent people were either rejected by traditional educational programmes or felt education simply had nothing to offer them. It is these people who initially come to APL cautiously but who often reap the most benefit.

The impact APL has had on the colleges themselves has been significant. They have had to address new issues related to admission, assessment, staff development and organisational structure. Once they know the strengths of their incoming or potential students, for example, it falls on them to design courses of study or learning opportunities that build on what the students already know. No longer does it make sense, for example, to simply send a student on a two-year course in business studies when college staff are convinced that the student already knows and can demonstrate more than half the course curriculum! This is but one of the challenges now facing further education colleges as they begin to embed APL as part of their normal provision.

Unemployed people
The diagnostic aspects of APL are also being used with the long-term unemployed in a variety of contexts. Again, the notion is that if we know what a person is already capable of doing, we can design training programmes better suited to the needs of that individual.

Many of the basic principles of APL are being applied during initial assessments and in conjunction with other forms of psychometric and skills testing. Significantly, in both Britain and the USA, unemployed people undergoing the process routinely report how much they have valued the opportunity to identify all they know and can do. Not surprisingly, improved self-confidence, so necessary to breaking the cycle of unemployment, has been a natural outcome for many people completing the process.

Training and Enterprise Councils

'Training and Enterprise Councils (TECs) have been created to unlock the potential of individuals, companies and communities across England and Wales' (ED,1991). One of their main aims is to raise the local skills base and spur business growth. They are directed by top business and community leaders with government funding, although it is expected that they will ultimately be able to generate a large percentage of their own income. Currently there are 82 TECs in England and Wales and another 22 Learning and Enterprise Companies (LECs) in Scotland.

One of the TECs' current priorities is to enable as many people as possible to obtain National Vocational Qualifications (NVQs). To do this, each TEC needs to set up a local network of assessors and various arrangements by which people can actually be assessed. Intrinsic to this work is the need for local trainers, educators and assessors to identify what individuals know and can do so that valuable training resources are not used to re-teach people what they already know and can do and to ensure that individuals are motivated to complete requirements for NVQs. APL has been built in to the TECs' work in this area. This effort involves not just training educational providers but also local employers, who in many cases provide the experts who serve as assessors.

This work by the TECs is an attempt to integrate APL in all training and educational offerings throughout the nation, bringing the benefits of APL to as many people as possible.

Summary

The accreditation of prior learning process, regardless of the terms used to describe it, is based on long-accepted theories and principles of experiential learning. It enables people, regardless of personal background, to demonstrate what they know and can do, and is of significant benefit to both individuals and organisations. Stemming from early work undertaken in the USA, the movement has been taken forward in a number of different ways in Britain, and is now developing further in Australia, Canada and elsewhere.

In the USA, APL has been developed largely in the context of higher education and for purposes of credit. In Britain it was originally introduced to provide an alternative route to higher education for adults but it is now being applied with a wide range of candidates, from experienced managers to the long-term unemployed, for a number of different purposes.

Chapter 2

The Role of Professionals in Delivering APL

The implementation of APL requires the involvement of many different kinds of people who bring to the process a wide range of professional skills and knowledge. It also requires that people work effectively not just as isolated individuals but as a team. This chapter reviews the various functions required to deliver an APL service. But before describing these, it is important to understand the basic APL model itself.

The APL model

The basic model of APL contains six stages, each having a set of specific objectives and activities (see Figure 2.1). Although APL can serve as a stand-alone service, evidence suggests that it is more effective when integrated with other learning, training and assessment options. Since APL is a *process*, not a specific assessment *measure*, additional assessment alternatives need to be available. Certain stages of the model, however, are useful for more than one purpose, as is described subsequently.

Stage 1: Pre-entry

During the pre-entry stage of APL, the organisation providing the service disseminates information to attract potential candidates. More specifically, it lets people know the service exists,

28

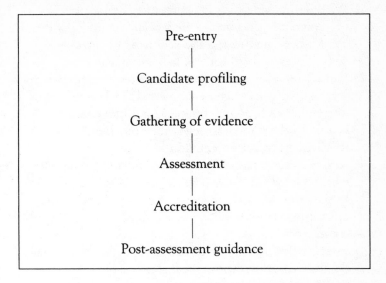

Figure 2.1 *The six stages of the APL model*

gives insight into the process and in some cases links the APL service to other services on offer. The primary objective of this stage is to give candidates adequate information to decide whether or not they wish to undergo the process.

Pre-entry activities include distributing brochures, producing press releases, meeting with groups of employers or any of a whole range of other strategies that are used to market services and products and disseminate information.

Stage 2: Candidate profiling

During this stage, candidates reflect on their experiences and accomplishments and begin to develop a profile of what they know and can do. It is also during this stage that candidates clarify their expectations in seeking recognition of their learning and equate what they know and can do with the standards or learning outcomes of a particular programme or qualification.

There are several activities that may occur during this stage to help candidates develop their profiles.

1. Working individually, candidates may complete a written or computer-generated self-assessment. Most often, checklists related to specific standards or learning outcomes form the basis for this self-assessment.
2. Candidates may also prepare a written description or personal report of what they know and can do across many different areas of accomplishment, and later compare this profile to the standards or learning outcomes in which they wish to receive recognition.
3. In some situations candidates may undergo an interview with a trained advisor to develop the necessary profile. In helping the candidate the advisor may use one or more checklists to help the candidate identify his or her areas of competence.
4. In still other situations, candidates may work in small groups to develop their individual profiles.

An organisation offering APL generally will provide one or more of these alternatives. Since a strong candidate profile is critical to the success of the APL process, it is important for APL providers to have clear and distinct ways of supporting candidates through this process. The clearer candidates are about their own strengths and how they relate to the standards or learning outcomes, the easier it is for them to collect the evidence they need.

Also during this stage, candidates need to receive information and guidance on the range of acceptable evidence needed to support their claims to credit. This includes receiving information on current assessment techniques that also may be applied, eg demonstration, oral or written questioning, etc.

Stage 3: Gathering and compiling of evidence

During this stage, candidates identify how they can best prove their competence or claim to credit and begin to collect the necessary evidence. Their task is to make sure they have sufficient and valid evidence to prove they really know and can do what they claim. The standards or learning outcomes serve as their guide.

During this stage, candidates undertake a range of activities:

- they may need to write to past or current employers for 'letters of validation' concerning their performance in the work place;
- they may need to gather from their place of work the products they have made or contributed to; and
- they may also need to generate new evidence to supplement the other forms of available evidence.

Once gathered, the evidence is then compiled or prepared for presentation. Most often this is in the form of a 'portfolio' or bound folder. It is important to add, however that not all evidence need be paper!

Also during this stage candidates prepare themselves for the actual assessment. Again, the APL organisation usually provides a range of different services to support candidates through this stage. Written guidelines, videos, group workshops, and one-to-one discussions – either in person or on the telephone – are all effective strategies.

Stage 4: Assessment

This stage is composed of several mini-stages.

1. The assessor first receives the portfolio and in a systematic fashion reviews it for completeness. He or she must be sure that the evidence relates to the standards or learning outcomes being claimed by the candidate and that there are no gaps in the evidence.
2. The assessor then needs to decide whether the evidence presented is sufficient; that is, does it provide full and ample proof that the standards or learning outcomes have been met?
3. If the assessor believes the evidence is sufficient, then no further assessment would be required and the assessor can

31

record the outcome, recommending credit or some other form of recognition. If the assessor believes that the evidence is *not* sufficient, however, he or she will need to develop an assessment plan.

4. Once the assessment plan is in place, it needs to be communicated to and agreed with the candidate. Assuming the candidate agrees, final arrangements for the assessment can be made.

5. The assessor then assesses the candidate using one or more different methods of assessment.

6. The assessor provides feedback to the candidate.

7. Lastly, the assessor records the outcomes of the assessment and transmits it to the appropriate administrative or academic office.

Stage 5: Accreditation

Depending on the context in which APL is being used, this stage will require action by the designated office actually responsible for awarding the credit or recognising the positive outcomes of the assessment. For example, within the context of further education in the UK, the national awarding bodies actually credit the candidate. Within the university context, however, it is the institution itself.

Stage 6: Post-assessment guidance

This final stage of the process underscores the developmental nature of APL. After assessment (and hopefully accreditation), candidates need to reflect on what they have achieved and review how their accomplishments relate to their initial expectations and goals. For many candidates this final stage helps to integrate what has been learned during the APL process with the candidate's overall personal and professional targets. It also serves to enhance the candidate's self-confidence and often motivates him or her to seek new learning and development goals.

Usually it is the trained advisor who provides this post-assessment guidance. In many programmes, it is also the advisor who gathers candidate feedback on the process, thereby providing the organisation with regular and on-going formative evaluation information.

Functions and roles of staff

Functions

For each of the six stages outlined above, there are many broad functions that need to be carried out to run a successful APL programme. These include:

- Marketing
- Informing
- Advising
- Advocating
- Setting standards
- Assessing
- Keeping records
- Providing feedback
- Evaluating
- Facilitating learning
- Managing

Who actually performs these functions will vary from one institution to the next, but it is essential that an organisation determine the nature of each required function in its own context. An organisation uncertain about these functions will be unable to identify effectively the most appropriate people to carry out the various roles and responsibilities needed to introduce APL.

Many of the functions cited above are offered primarily by the APL advisors and assessors and these are described in detail in subsequent chapters. What follows, however, is a brief description of some of the key functions provided by others within an organisation which are also needed to implement a viable APL service, namely, marketing, informing, setting standards, keeping records, facilitating learning and managing.

Marketing

Not so many years ago, colleges and universities rejected the concept of marketing. They may have 'disseminated' information, 'recruited' students, 'lobbied' for more money, but certainly did not undertake marketing – that was something only business and industry did! Now, of course, most organisations, whether in the public or private sector, market their goods and services – academic and training providers included.

On one level marketing an APL service is no different from marketing any other service. The range of marketing strategies may well be the same. Brochures, posters, newspaper articles and advertisements, public presentations and so forth are all useful possibilities. But there are many significant differences. Recognising and effectively dealing with these differences can well mean the difference between an organisation's success and failure in implementing APL.

Language
One significant difference in marketing an APL service is the language itself. 'Accreditation of prior learning' or any of the other words that have been developed to describe the process simply do not make sense to the majority of people, regardless of nation or language spoken! The concept may be clear to professionals but it simply is not to the general public, even to those people who might serve to benefit the most from the service. It is therefore *essential* that the concept be marketed using plain and understandable words. (In frustration, one college, unable to find agreement among its staff as to what its APL programme should be called, came up with a single phrase: 'George'. They then geared their marketing strategy around words such as, 'Can George help?', 'Do you know who George is?', 'George can give you credit. Call us . . .', etc. Although some people thought this was a highly effective, innovative approach,

others (including an accrediting organisation) thought it was silly, certainly not descriptive of the service on offer, and perhaps most importantly, demeaning to the candidates actually coming forward for the service. Such are the problems of seeking creative solutions to difficult problems!)

In the UK, a number of organisations are moving to phrases like 'Crediting Competence' which serve to link APL with the whole move to competency-based qualifications. But again many potential candidates may not think they are 'competent'. They may think they have 'skills' and 'knowledge' but even here, there may be exceptions. For example, people suffering from very low self-esteem, like many long-term unemployed and others disadvantaged, may believe they have no skills or knowledge. If they did, why have they been unemployed for so long? They may, however, think in terms of what they can do or have done.

Getting the language right is of critical importance to promote APL effectively. It also means that to market APL well, an organisation needs to target particular candidate groups. Once it knows the primary targets, often the appropriate language becomes obvious.

Expectations
Another serious marketing issue that needs to be addressed is the level of expectation that the advertising creates. Many APL services during their development period make the mistake of promising more than they can deliver. They are so anxious to get people in the door that they create false hopes. Potential candidates come *expecting* that they will automatically receive recognition or credit for what they can do and leave disappointed to have learned that (a) the process is not automatic or easy and (b) that in many instances what they know and can do is not appropriate or even relevant to the organisation offering the service. The marketing has to encourage potential candidates but not be misleading.

Individuals or organisations?
In many APL programmes throughout the world, initial market-

ing efforts have been directed at individuals in the community. Some continue in this direction, although increasingly, as employers and others become more involved and committed to fostering better educated and trained workers, organisations offering APL have focused their efforts on particularly receptive employers, unions or community agencies. This often leads to highly successful joint ventures in which both organisations gain considerably. Often, APL providers find that they make better use of their resources if they work in this way with one or more organisations.

A *separate or integrated service?*

The notion of joint ventures raises yet another critical issue. Should the APL service be promoted separately or along with the range of other services and programmes offered by the organisation? The answer depends on a number of factors:

1. Does the providing organisation have an overall policy for APL or is the service going to be limited to one or two vocational or academic disciplines?
2. Organisationally, *can* APL be integrated? That is, have staff been given the necessary time and training to perform the various advising and assessing functions?
3. Are there clear links or progression points between APL and other services and programmes within the organisation?

Many organisations initially promote APL as a separate entity. This serves to raise awareness within the potential candidate groups and gives the organisation a framework in which to implement and evaluate its APL service. With experience, however, most then move to integrate the marketing of APL with other related services or programmes. The more successful APL programmes choose to do a bit of both. For example, they may describe their APL service in all of their general information, but then produce special leaflets, brochures and support materials to provide greater detail about the process and its benefits.

Credibility

Credibility is perhaps the biggest APL marketing issue of all. Even though the concept of APL has been around a long time, its implementation in current-day training and educational organisations is new. Many people, including the candidates coming forward for the service, want to know if the credit, qualifications or other recognition they receive, is as 'good' as more traditional ones. Many adult learners long by-passed by the educational and training system, view education, training and qualifications as valuable only to someone 'smarter or more clever than I am'. Similarly, they often place teachers, lecturers, professors or anyone else within an academic or training organisation on a very high pedestal. It is no wonder that they often have difficulty accepting that what they have learned informally or maybe even accidentally is equal to what goes in the more hallowed halls of learning. And it is not just by-passed learners who question the credibility of APL. There are also professional teachers or trainers who may believe that, 'If you haven't learned it from me, you haven't learned it', or, 'If you didn't learn it the way I learned it, it can't be very good'.

Attitudes such as these need to be addressed as part of an *internal* marketing strategy. Frequently, people who hold these views have not really thought about the implications of what they hold to be true. Sometimes it is useful to point out that all over the world there are competent biologists, hairdressers, doctors, historians, automobile mechanics, computer specialists and so forth and that everyone has learned in different ways, been exposed to different theories and ways of doing things and certainly has been assessed by different people in many diverse settings. Who is to judge that any one way is truly better than any other?

All of these issues relate to the marketing function of APL providers. As may be obvious, the marketing of APL cannot be assumed only by the public relations department. It is a function that needs to be integrated throughout the organisation and fostered by many different people. APL marketing is also not just about recruiting potential users to the service; often significant marketing needs to be done within the organisation as well.

Informing

A second important function required of an APL service is providing information. All candidates need information to begin the APL process. But consider the range of information they need *during* the process. They need to know, for example:

1. how the process works at each stage;
2. the range of advice and support on offer;
3. the roles and responsibilities of the people to be involved;
4. the support materials available;
5. the schedule of workshops or briefing sessions;
6. the hours the organisation is accessible;
7. the office hours of the advisor and assessor;
8. qualifications on offer;
9. fees;
10. time frames for each stage of the process;
11. how and when they will receive feedback;
12. how their credits (or other recognition) will be recorded and so forth.

They also need insight on the nature of acceptable evidence and assessment; and they need to know and be able to interpret the standards or learning outcomes on offer. Candidates and potential candidates are not the only ones who need information. Employers, union representatives, community service agencies, all of these need to know about APL. The function of 'informing', therefore, is another critical component in implementing an APL service.

Who should do the informing?

Staff who have particular roles within the APL process, namely advisors and assessors, provide a lot of the information candidates require. Their roles are fully described in subsequent chapters. But they are not alone in helping candidates and others receive needed information about the APL service. All staff who serve as points of contact within an organisation or who represent the organisation in public forums can fulfil an informing function.

For example, it is often a well-trained receptionist, secretary or switchboard operator who can make the difference between a satisfied or complaining customer. People in such positions need to be trained as effectively as assessors: that is not to say that they need to know the *same* things, but they do need to be able to positively respond to enquiries, perhaps provide basic information about the APL service and offer the names of other institutional contacts. All too often the 'support' people within an organisation are ignored or minimally trained to respond to people's requests for information about a new service. The results, as many organisations have learned the hard way, can be disastrous. Consider, for example, the college that failed to tell the switchboard operators what the letters 'APL' stood for. When a potential candidate telephoned and asked for the 'accreditation of prior learning' office, the switchboard office was emphatic that no such office existed!

In addition, it is not only 'support' people and those with specific roles and responsibilities in APL who need to know details about the APL service. It is anyone within an organisation who might be asked a question by a potential candidate, an employer or government policy maker, including senior managers. Everyone within an organisation – from senior manager to clerical assistant – should be able to provide the information requested or point the caller in the right direction. This is part of a Total Quality Management approach. An institution offering APL needs to consider the many ways in which such information can best be provided and by whom.

Setting standards

As is highlighted in Chapter 1, the UK government has committed itself to the development of national occupational standards of competence. These national standards serve as the basis for the new National Vocational Qualifications (NVQs; SVQs in Scotland). The new qualifications are offered through a number of national awarding bodies such as the City & Guilds of London Institute (CGLI) and the Business and Technician Education Council (BTEC). Learners work towards and obtain these new qualifications in school/further/higher education, in employment, independently or some combination.

Since very few, if any other nations, have fully committed themselves to the development of standards in this way, most organisations wishing to offer an APL service need to set standards. The process of setting standards becomes a prerequisite to offering the full service. Whether the standards are called 'learning outcomes' or 'competence-based standards' or anything else, it is imperative that clear statements are in place and that all those involved in the APL process – candidates, advisors, assessors and subsequent trainers or teachers – understand and can use the standards. It is impossible to assess candidates without an agreed standard by which to assess them. Keeping in mind that one of the key principles of APL is that it permits assessment *not linked to any particular learning or training programme*, it is essential that clear, assessable standards are developed.

Where there are no 'national' or externally defined standards, developing the standards is primarily the responsibility of subject specialists within a given institution or context, eg, a university department, a professional association, or industrial sector. Often these are the same people who serve as assessors. It is their job to determine the assessable outcomes of their training or academic programmes. Minimally they need to ask:

- 'What is it we expect our trainees, students or employees to be able to do and know?' and
- 'To what standard and in what contexts do we expect them to be able to demonstrate that they have these skills and knowledge?'

An example may be helpful. In this example, taken from the Management 1 standards of the Management Charter Initiative, (MCI, 1991) in the UK, one activity expected of a competent manager is to:

Set and update work objectives for teams and individuals.

Although this statement sets out the activity – the element of competence, as it's termed – it does not specify the performance criteria against which the manager could be judged. The performance criteria attached to this activity are as follows:

1. Objectives are clear, accurate, and contain all relevant details including measures of performance.
2. Achievement of the objectives is practicable within the set period given other work commitments.
3. Objectives are explained in sufficient detail and in a manner, and at a level and pace appropriate to all the relevant individuals.
4. Objectives are updated regularly with the relevant individuals to take into account individual, team and organisational changes.
5. Individuals are encouraged to seek clarification of any areas of which they are unsure.

These standards also include specifications for knowledge and understanding, eg, principles and methods relating to establishing, defining and reviewing objectives and performance measures; defining and allocating responsibilities and authority. Also included is an indication of the range of conditions under which the performance should meet the standard and/or other delineation of range. Always the focus is on the outcomes: what we expect people to be able to know and do regardless of how they learned it.

Standards, it is important to add, can also be set for those traits and capabilities sometimes called personal effectiveness traits. There are many different models that have already been derived covering a range of traits such as leadership, planning, and initiative (Astin *et al.*, 1986) and extending to statements like 'striving for improvement', 'making decisions', 'showing sensitivity to others', etc. (Simosko, 1990b). Here too, groups of professionals needed to decide what they meant by 'personal effectiveness' and once agreed they needed to develop criteria by which to judge the individuals under consideration.

Methods to set standards
There are many acceptable methods by which subject experts can work together to spell out what is it they expect learners to achieve and demonstrate. Some of the methods include DACUM, Delphi, functional analysis and others. All are based on gathering information about a particular occupation or field of study from those who are most knowledgeable. Some such as DACUM and functional analysis bring people together to work in groups. Others, such as Delphi, rely on survey methods in which participants learn the opinions of others but are not able to engage in discussion and debate. Each system has its strengths and limitations. Professionals needing to develop standards would be wise to consult a range of source documents, most often available in reference libraries.

Further, those developing standards may be required or want to work with external organisations who can serve to 'validate' the usefulness or appropriateness of the standards – or any emerging qualifications based on those standards. In the UK, for example, the National Council for Vocational Qualifications serves to validate qualifications based on the standards developed by lead-industry bodies.

Keeping records

Good record-keeping is another key function of a successful APL process. It is a process many people take for granted. To implement APL effectively, however, most organisations find they need to reconsider their current procedures, sometimes making significant modifications or additions to accommodate the needs of APL candidates. Record-keeping takes place at each stage of the APL process and involves not only the specific activities described below but also the organisation of a sound *system* for the storage and retrieval of records. This overall system needs to be evaluated regularly and modified to suit the changing needs of the organisation and the people who provide the service.

Pre-entry
At the pre-entry phase most organisations try to maintain a list of people who write or telephone for information. They also maintain files of any potential candidates who attend briefing seminars or workshops. Since most potential candidates also complete application forms, APL centres must take care to collect the information that will be most useful in guiding the candidate through the system and have a systematic way of processing those application forms.

Profiling
At the second stage, profiling the candidate, there are additional record-keeping responsibilities. If advisors are working with candidates on a one-to-one basis, the outcomes of each session should to be recorded and, following recommended procedures, shared and agreed with the candidate. The nature of the information recorded will vary but at the very least it should specify:

1. the reasons the candidate is seeking the recognition;
2. any qualifications or portions of qualifications the candidate is seeking;
3. the actual 'profile' of the candidate, whether in checklist or sketched-out narrative form;
4. likely sources of evidence for the candidate; and
5. an agreed plan of action, eg, an assessment or learning contract or the date for the next meeting with the advisor, etc.

Gathering of evidence

While the candidate is actually gathering his or her evidence during the third stage of the APL process, the APL centre will want to record the outcomes of any telephone or written enquiries made by the candidate. In addition, if there are on-going portfolio development workshops, notes of a candidate's progress should also be recorded, always, of course, with the candidate's knowledge and approval. The reasons for keeping such careful records of a candidate's progress is not to monitor the candidate *per se* but to provide as much helpful guidance and support as possible. This is especially true if more than one staff member is to be involved with the candidate prior to assessment. For example, a candidate may attend a weekly portfolio development workshop facilitated by one advisor but then telephone his or her own advisor at a later date for clarification about some other matter. Careful records can ensure that candidates receive consistent information and, of course, from the centre's point of view, problem areas are more easily identified.

Assessment

The assessment stage requires the highest demands on the record-keeping function:

1. Assessment plans must be carefully spelled out and agreed with the candidate.
2. The outcomes of each assessment must be carefully recorded.
3. Candidates must receive written and clear statements regarding the outcomes of their assessment.
4. Summary information required by third parties such as registrars or verifiers must be clear and comprehensive.
5. Administrative records need to be carefully completed to provide an accurate historical perspective of the candidate's assessment. For example, it would be essential for the record to indicate the date(s) of the assessment, the names of the assessor(s), the outcomes of the

assessment, and the date and nature of the candidate's award.

Post-assessment guidance
This last stage of the process provides a good opportunity to review with candidates the records compiled on them during the APL process, especially if careful notes have been kept about the candidates' original objectives. Often candidates are very pleasantly surprised to see how far they have come in meeting their initial target. Reviewing it with the advisor helps to reinforce and integrate all that the candidate has thus far achieved.

Most advisors also record any future plans the candidate may have set for him or herself, again to have a complete picture should the candidate return to the centre for additional support or assistance.

Facilitating learning

Although this book is about assessing and recognising people's prior learning, there is no doubt that an important function of most centres offering APL is that of providing new opportunities for learning. Most people coming forward of their own accord for APL are interested in their own development, and that usually includes learning something more. Whether in a college, university or employment setting, APL providers need to consider how they will help people develop themselves.

For many APL providers, namely colleges and universities, this looks like a simple enough matter to deal with. If you can recognise an individual's learning achievements, so the thinking goes, you can simply place the candidate on the next level of instruction, exempting him or her from the lower-level material. On paper this seems like a reasonable approach and indeed in many colleges and universities, particularly in North America, this is the way APL works. Along with exemption, many candidates also receive academic awards towards an end qualification, eg, a degree.

In truth most people do not learn in the way in which traditional course offerings are devised. They master a bit of one and a bit of another and perhaps do not have sufficient evidence for any single course or unit. For other adults, the situation is even more complicated than that. Many adult learners have a wide variety of experience and are well able to demonstrate or prove what they can do. What they often lack, however, is the theoretical or underpinning knowledge also expected in many traditional academic programmes.

This poses a number of problems for the APL centre. How can it formally recognise or accredit an individual's achievements when those achievements reflect only a portion of what is expected in the course or learning programme?

In the UK, with its history of one- and two-year courses, one solution is to divide the course into smaller units – modularise the curriculum. This process is indeed well underway in further education in response to the move to NVQs and many institutions of higher education are also beginning to 'unitise' their curriculum. The modularisation of the curriculum based on standards of competence or learning outcomes will significantly enhance the development and use of APL. Unit-based qualifications with clear and assessable standards mean that it will be relatively easy for candidates to equate their learning to the standards and gather the necessary evidence for assessment. For the centre, it will be easier and more cost effective to assess the candidate and most importantly, provide the necessary additional learning or training required by the candidate.

Open and flexible learning

Many providers of APL offer traditional educational or training programmes. In some cases APL candidates can make use of these; in others they cannot because of work or family commitments. Increasingly, however, traditional educational and training providers who also wish to offer APL are introducing open and flexible learning alternatives for their candidates.

For some candidates – those who are self-reliant, well motivated and fully literate – these are exciting, viable options. For other candidates, however, distance or open learning will be of limited value. These candidates may need other, more structured and supported learning options, to meet their overall goals.

Costs

Cost is another factor APL centres need to consider as they investigate using distance or open learning options. One APL candidate in the field of information technology found that to obtain all the open learning packages he would have needed to 'top up' his learning, would have cost over £1000, when the actual traditional cost was well under £300! This particular candidate felt 'between the devil and the deep blue sea'. As he put it, 'On the one hand, I already know and can do a lot of what is required to meet the standards, but admittedly, not everything. But I'm also not prepared to give up my job to take the full day-time course or spend £1000 to get the little I need. Surely, there must be another option'.

For candidates like this one, a suitable option may well be 'flexible' or 'self-paced' workshops offered in the evenings or at the weekends by the APL provider. As some centres are demonstrating, properly designed, these workshops can allow large numbers of candidates to learn and progress at their own pace with support provided by peers and a limited number of paid professional tutors or trainers.

Centres offering APL may have a number of other ideas for providing learning opportunities. The important point is that the learning options need to be flexible, of real value to the candidate and appropriate to his or her unique learning needs.

Managing

APL, like all other programmes, needs to be managed. And it needs to be managed by a named individual having a range of responsibilities and resources available. The person needs to have a staff to carry out the various functions required of the service, eg, advising, assessing, providing information, recording, etc, and a range of resources, eg, a physical location in which to offer the service, written support materials, etc.

The APL manager must be a very able manager of people

because central to the success of any APL service is a strong APL team. No one person can offer an APL service. There must be a clear delineation of roles and responsibilities and the manager must facilitate an effective team approach to make the system work.

Total Quality Management (TQM)
There are many lessons to be learned from applying a TQM approach to APL. At the heart of the TQM approach is a redefinition of the word 'quality'. Not so long ago, quality referred to luxury or high-cost items. Today, quality means putting the customer first, and that means:

- identifying who the customers are;
- finding out what they want; and
- providing that in the most cost effective and helpful way possible.

Applied to APL, a centre must identify the potential users of the service, learn what they need and expect of the centre and then seek to provide all the necessary information, support, guidance, assessment and learning services that will satisfy the needs of the users.

To offer a full, viable APL service, the centre must involve every employee in some way in the process, creating a strong team approach. Each team member should be trained to deliver some aspect(s) of the APL service. More importantly they should be pleasant to the customers and flexible in their approach. The centre will want to offer a range of flexible assessment and learning options for users (whether individual candidates or other organisations) and make sure each and every user, or potential user, feels welcome and valued. In addition, there must be visible signs that the senior management is fully committed to adequately resourcing and marketing the service and drawing on the ideas of the staff for continuous improvement. The case study provided below will highlight the way in which an organisation might use the concept of TQM to introduce APL.

Case Study

A TQM Approach to APL

- *Identifying customer requirements*

A local college with declining enrolments decided to approach a number of local companies to find out if they could be of service. Senior managers from both sectors set up a local forum in which mutual concerns could be discussed and issues addressed. At the very first meeting, some of the employers reported a series of problems:

1. They were having to retrain a number of recent graduates who lacked the necessary skills and knowledge to work effectively.
2. They were paying high fees for professional trainers to offer in-company courses similar to the ones offered by the college.
3. They were trying to recruit people who seemed to have the necessary skills and knowledge but no qualifications indicative of their performance.
4. Within each company there were middle managers and technicians who seemed unable or unwilling to progress or adapt within the company but who were too valued to be made redundant.

- *Satisfying customer needs*

The college management and staff set about developing possible strategies aimed at satisfying these customer needs. They came up with a number of ideas:

1. Auditing the curriculum with help from industry representatives.
2. Developing a new curriculum based on standards set by college staff and representatives of industry.
3. Introducing an APL service which would allow people to earn credit for what they knew and could do.
4. Expanding the opening hours of the college so employees could make use of the college before and after work and at weekends.

5. Introducing open and distance learning options as well as flexible learning workshops or forums, some of which would be held on the company's premises.
6. Modifying admission procedures so that everyone has an opportunity to profile his or her strengths and interests before progressing on a new learning programme.
7. Developing a staff training programme for the college which would make each person more responsive to the needs of both external and internal customers.

● *Providing customer service*
The management of the college endorsed the idea of these changes and began working with a number of different teams whose objectives were:

1. to establish whether or not the college could provide these services, and
2. if they could, how they were to facilitate the necessary changes.

● *Commitment to training*
A major part of the implementation plan was a commitment to staff training on three levels:

1. an awareness programme of what total quality means in relation to self and customers;
2. advice on organisational changes that must take place in order to 'put the customer first'; and
3. specialist training for individuals in order that they could function within the new set up, eg, specific roles within the APL service.

● *Measuring success*
The dramatic increase in enrolments was the most obvious short-term measure of success. The new enrolments came from three main areas:

1. Existing employees from local companies came on part-time courses which were *now* comparable with the courses being offered by in-company trainers.
2. New employees in many local companies, who had no formal

qualifications but had experience enrolled for and acquired qualifications through the college APL service.

3. Learners from the local community were now able to enrol on courses due to the new flexible approach of the college, particularly with APL which opened up many opportunities for the adult population.

Success of the TQM approach to APL was not only measured through the increase in enrolments. A much broader and longer-term effect was in relation to staff attitudes throughout the college. Every employee, from the switchboard operators to senior managers had undergone some form of staff development or training. This not only increased people's sense of worth in the college but had a positive effect on the college's dealings with the public in offering an APL service.

Obviously, this case study only serves to highlight how a TQM approach could be used to introduce an APL service. It may not always be possible to undertake such an extensive programme. However, one of the key components of TQM – satisfying the needs of the customer – must be integral to any APL service, if it is to be truly learner-centred.

Summary

The basic APL model contains six stages, which are not necessarily discrete: pre-entry, candidate profiling, gathering of evidence, assessment, accreditation, and post-assessment guidance. Each one of the stages requires a number of people with different skills to carry out a wide range of functions, ranging from initial marketing to managing and evaluating the APL programme. Assessors, advisors, APL coordinators and all other involved staff have to work both individually and as part of a team in order to run a successful APL programme.

Identifying and satisfying the needs of the customer is the cornerstone of Total Quality Management (TQM). If APL is to be truly flexible and responsive to learner needs, it also must be about satisfying the needs of the customer. It is therefore clear that a TQM approach to APL is an excellent starting point in planning and implementing an APL service.

Chapter 3

Advising, Mentoring, Supporting

APL, as we have seen in Chapter 2, is a learner-centred service. It is designed to 'put the customer first' and help each candidate to meet his or her individual goals. All candidates, however, no matter how well motivated, require information, encouragement and advice as they progress through the APL process. Some do fine with a minimum of help and support, others require a lot of attention and creative mentoring.

In this chapter we will look at the role of the advisor in supporting and mentoring candidates through the APL process. We identify the primary responsibilities of the advisor, describe effective ways of working with candidates, and offer some helpful hints in setting up a range of APL advising services.

Role of the advisor

The role of the advisor in APL is primarily that of mentor, a 'wise and trusted guide' (Hanks, 1988). The APL advisor serves as the candidate's advocate and offers information, advice and guidance. In fulfilling this role the advisor's most essential purpose is to help empower candidates, thereby enabling them to assume increasing responsibility for themselves and to make sound decisions.

Reflecting

One of the primary outcomes of the second stage of the APL process is the development of a profile that portrays what a candidate knows and can do. Sometimes candidates are able to develop these profiles on their own using a variety of self-assessment tools, but most often they need some form of help or encouragement. For many candidates this help comes from the APL advisor whose main task is to help the candidate reflect on experiences and accomplishments which will enable the candidate to develop a comprehensive profile of his or her strengths and abilities.

Many candidates come to the APL process believing that they have very little 'creditable' learning. There is a tendency for them, especially those who are a bit unsure of themselves, to discount much of what they know and can do. It is the role of the advisor to help candidates 'lift the canopy' from their often limited self-perceptions and damning self-appraisals.

Advisors do this in many different ways. The more effective ones:

- gain the trust and confidence of the candidates;
- are active listeners;
- give useful and sensitive feedback;
- ask relevant questions;
- suggest new ways of seeing things; and
- link apparently disparate ideas or facts and offer these for the candidate's consideration.

Active learners

Candidates also need to be encouraged to reflect on themselves *as learners*. Many adults will acknowledge that they know and can do something but they will not readily admit to being *actively engaged in the learning process itself*. As they begin their APL work, adults regularly view learning as a passive or unconscious function. How many APL advisors have asked a candidate, 'When and how did you learn to do that?' only to hear, 'Oh, I don't know. I guess I picked it up somewhere', or 'I think I just was lucky; someone showed me a thing or two,' or 'Everyone knows and can do that ... nothing special about that!' The advisor has a unique opportunity to help the individual see him or herself as someone who has *control* over what has been or could be or will be learned. Giving the learner control is perhaps the most profound way of 'putting the customer first'.

As was pointed out in Chapter 1, much of what we all learn seems to be unconscious and many of the skills we possess are acquired seemingly accidentally. Yet on reflection, it is often possible to see that perhaps the process of learning was not as unconscious or as accidental as it seemed. When people really have an opportunity to review and consider how they have come to know or do something, they often see that circumstances, motivation and their relationships with others have each played a critical role in the acquisition of their skills and knowledge. They also come to see that to a very large degree they were actively involved in solving problems, making choices, allocating resources, etc at the very time they were 'accidentally' learning something.

Although APL is a tool used by a wide variety of people to receive formal recognition or credit for their skills, knowledge and abilities, it can also serve as a valuable opportunity for personal development. It is important for APL advisors to be aware of this aspect of the process and to foster, as often as possible, the notion of 'active learning'. Active learners are more inclined to take greater responsibility for themselves, to demonstrate a higher level of self-confidence and to value education and training. Surely these characteristics are central to the goals and activities of all professionals who are in the training or education business, particularly those charged with the role of advising, mentoring or supporting others.

Advising, not telling

APL advising requires each advisor to find the right balance between 'telling' and 'advising'. And indeed, it is often a delicate balance to find. The advisor who helps his or her candidates by telling them what to do may be very problem-centred. But often in focusing on the problem, the advisor excludes the candidates from the problem-solving process, thereby denying them the opportunity to take greater responsibility for themselves (De Board, 1989).

APL advising requires that the advisor address the candidate's particular needs in gaining recognition for his or her achievements and help the candidate to understand the details of the process. To help the candidate understand the APL process, a significant part of the advisor's responsibility is to 'inform' the candidate, provide all of the current and accurate information the candidate needs, clarify the roles of the various people with whom the candidate will interact, describe the support services available and so forth. In the context of APL, information is power.

It is also essential, of course, that the advisor addresses the unique problems or hurdles that confront the candidate. A competent advisor will get as many facts and details about the candidate as possible and, based on that information, develop a number of options and alternatives for the candidate to consider. This is especially true, for example, when candidates are trying to identify the various types of evidence they might (or might not) be able to obtain.

Mentoring, not protecting

As a mentor, the APL advisor must also encourage candidates to set out their own strategies and solutions to problems that emerge during the APL process. Keeping in mind the 'wise and trusted guide' definition, the advisor must try to support the candidate to take full responsibility for his or her own actions and quietly withdraw to the background as the candidate gains self-confidence and a sense of purpose. It is the wise advisor, indeed, who lets go at the right time.

APL advisors, however, like the mentor in Dante's *Divine Comedy*, also need to alert candidates to potential hazards and pitfalls. This is as much a part of the informing role as describing the role of the assessor or any other aspect of the process. As the mentor, the advisor should *want* the candidate to succeed with as little red tape and difficulty as possible. But the advisor also must remember that he or she cannot protect the candidate from making mistakes, feeling discouraged or not earning the recognition the candidate seeks. Ultimately, it is the candidate who is responsible for his or her own success or lack of it in APL, not the advisor.

A resource, not a clinical counsellor

Serving as an APL advisor is not always an easy role to assume. There is often a tendency for new advisors to want to get too involved in the particular circumstances of an individual's life, to rescue the candidate in some way. By listening to the life stories which often emerge as part of candidates' reflections, advisors are frequently moved by a deep and profound desire to help candidates out of what may be painful or dangerous life situations.

For many candidates, the APL process offers a first-time opportunity to actually talk about themselves in detail with someone genuinely listening. Even though the main purpose of meeting with an APL advisor is to help the candidates develop profiles that can be used to seek formal recognition or credit, it is inevitable that other details of the candidate's life also will emerge. For example, in describing how she came to own her own successful business, one woman painfully relived with her APL advisor the family circumstances that led her into a period of dire economic poverty which forced her to completely alter her life. She began crying and had difficulty getting control of herself.

Using common sense, the APL advisor got the woman a warm drink and some tissues and waited for her to regain her composure. The advisor then dealt with the situation in a warm and gentle way by acknowledging the pain the woman obviously was feeling and asking if she would like to continue the APL work or return for another appointment.

What the APL advisor *did not* attempt to do was delve into the woman's past, analyse her problems or offer therapeutic support. It may be that at a later date, if the opportunity presented itself or the matter arose again, the APL advisor might be able to let the woman know about a local counselling facility and leave the decision about whether to use it to the candidate herself. In this and other contexts, APL advisors serve as valuable resources to their candidates. Ideally they are familiar with local services and networks in their communities and can provide important information and referrals that will enable candidates to receive the assistance or information they might need – quite unrelated to the APL process itself.

APL advisors, however, are not therapeutic counsellors or psychotherapists. It is not their job to solve candidates' personal or psychological problems. Putting aside all the obvious ethical and legal implications, attempting to provide a psychological service, rather than one that is basically educational, could be extremely damaging to the candidates *and* their well-meaning advisors.

Supporting, not building false expectations

APL advisors serve as the candidates' contact and support throughout the APL process. APL advisors, then, have yet another important responsibility: to support and motivate the candidate but not create false expectations that will set the candidate up for failure or disappointment. This requires another delicate balance.

Most experienced advisors quickly learn to be sensitive to the needs of their candidates and provide the type of support they need. For example, one advisor reported that every Monday morning she would receive a telephone call from one of her candidates. The candidate's purpose in calling was to tell her about the work he had completed on his portfolio over the weekend and to seek her approval for proceeding. The advisor said she was actually sorry when the candidate had completed his portfolio because his sense of enthusiasm and pride was often an inspiration to her, especially on Monday mornings! Clearly, for this candidate, the best support the advisor could provide was to (1) acknowledge and praise the candidate's progress, (2) respond to any questions he presented, and (3) offer encouragement for the next piece of work the candidate had to tackle.

By contrast, another candidate contacted the advisor infrequently and when she did so, it generally was out of a sense of obligation. To the advisor, the candidate seemed demotivated and unable to focus on the work for any extended period of time. Over the course of several months her advisor was able to offer five different types of support:

- he arranged to meet with her individually on several occasions to discuss particular problems she was having;
- he arranged for her to join a 'portfolio development group' of others who were developing their portfolios;
- he asked to review her work in small segments to give her on-going feedback, rather than wait until she had completed her entire portfolio;
- he also helped her to develop a realistic schedule for completing her work (taking into consideration her home and work responsibilities); and
- lastly, he discussed her unique issues regarding evidence with the assessor in order to give her the best guidance he could as she gathered and developed the necessary documentation for her portfolio.

As these examples illustrate, candidates vary in the amount and nature of the support they require. Advisors often have difficult decisions to make regarding the time and other resources they can offer to any given candidate. Early on in their relationship with the candidate, advisors need to spell out as clearly as possible the parameters of the support on offer and control any tendency some candidates may have to misuse the options available. For example, many advisors set particular hours each week for receiving candidates' telephone enquiries. Candidates who are unwilling or unable to telephone during those hours need to be helped to find alternative ways of communicating with the advisor. Although APL is very much a candidate-centred service, advisors have the right and responsibility to control their time, resources and support in keeping with the best practices of their organisation and profession.

Providing facts and figures

The role of the APL advisor is complex and requires a good deal of creativity and sensitivity. It also requires knowledge of all the facts and figures associated with the process. It is the advisor who must know and convey the costs, fees, and timetable of the service. It is also the advisor who will need to identify the location and office hours of others the candidate will see during the process, eg, the assessors, the registrar, etc. And it is the advisor who will introduce the details of the entire process to the candidate and provide technical guidance on such matters as assessment alternatives. Lastly, it is also the advisor who will explain the range of support services and materials on offer.

In most instances organisations prepare a lot of this inform-ation in written form. It can then be distributed to the candidate and reviewed as necessary with the advisor. For some candidates who have limited reading skills, of course, the advisor will need to provide the information orally.

Candidates will seek out advisors for all sorts of reasons, some related to APL, some not. Often an advisor will have just the answer or information the candidate needs but it is the wise advisor who recognises that he or she will not have all the answers all the time for all the candidates. And it is the *very* wise advisor – the one who puts the customer first – who sometimes guides the candidate in other, more appropriate directions.

Summary of advisor responsibilities

As may already be obvious, within this role, APL advisors have many responsibilities. They must be able to:

- encourage people to clarify goals, identify obstacles or issues and develop strategies for overcoming them;
- help candidates reflect on their past experiences and identify their strengths and accomplishments;
- assist candidates to develop a strong personal profile which is linked to the standards or course(s) against which the person wishes to be assessed;
- provide correct and adequate information which will enable candidates to make sound decisions;
- help candidates develop their portfolios of evidence and prepare for assessment;
- actively listen to candidates and provide appropriate feedback throughout the process;
- liaise with APL assessors and others on the APL team; and
- maintain accurate records.

The remainder of this chapter looks at how advisors can effectively meet all of these responsibilities for each candidate and do so in a calm and systematic way.

Effective ways of working with APL candidates

Most APL advisors find they need to develop a coherent framework or system for working with each candidate. This is the only way they can genuinely make sure that they provide a comparable service to all candidates and maintain necessary control of their own valuable time. The first part of this framework is often called the 'staged or structured interview'. As the name suggests, there are several different stages or steps within this model which enable the advisor and the candidate to

61

progress systematically during the profiling stage of the APL process and into the gathering of evidence stage.

The staged interview

The staged interview is generally divided into six distinct phases. These include:

1. Welcome and introduction.
2. Establishing the candidate's aims in seeking APL.
3. Reflecting on the candidate's experience and accomplishments.
4. Linking the candidate profile to the recognition or qualifications sought.
5. Matching specific skills and knowledge to the standards or learning outcomes specified in the qualifications.
6. Developing an action or assessment plan.

We will look in detail at each of these stages and describe the range of expected outcomes for each.

Stage 1: Welcome and introduction

As the name suggests, this stage often marks the real beginning of the APL process for many candidates. It may be the first time the candidate meets his or her advisor individually. (In some APL programmes, candidates may have the opportunity to attend a group briefing or orientation session at which they actually meet the APL advisors in a group situation.)

Although the words 'welcome' and 'introduction' seem simple enough, it is interesting to hear a group of professionals describe what they actually do during this stage. Good practice suggests that:

- candidates be greeted in such a way that allows them to know they were expected;
- advisors extend a smile, handshake and/or other informal greeting;
- advisors ask to be called by their first names; and

- advisors clarify with the candidate the name he or she wishes to be called.

It is essential that the candidate be encouraged to feel welcomed and that the environment seems well organised, pleasant and credible. Advisors should aim to create a friendly but business-like atmosphere. Some adults have reported feeling a bit intimidated at the beginning of the interview and then report how pleased they were to feel that they were dealing with a 'real person' who was taking them seriously. On the other hand, other adults have sometimes been put off by advisors who have tried a bit too hard to be friendly and establish instant rapport.

Clearly each advisor needs to use the words and mannerisms that best suit him or her. The outcome of this very brief, but critical, phase of the staged interview is to make the candidate feel comfortable and ready to begin.

Stage 2: Establishing the candidate's aims in seeking APL
The length of time required for this phase of the interview will vary from programme to programme and from candidate to candidate. Some candidates come to the interview very clear about their aims in seeking APL, others may be quite vague. It is up to the advisor to make sure by the end of this stage that candidates have clear and realistic expectations of the process.

To get to this outcome, it may be necessary for advisors to confirm that candidates have adequate knowledge and under-standing of the APL process itself. If the candidates have attended an APL briefing session or have received, read and understood written materials about the process, this may be a relatively simple matter. Some candidates, however, will need to have the advisor review the process in some detail before they can actually develop a clear picture for themselves. Organ-isations often produce written or other visual materials to help advisors explain the APL process, sometimes in more than one language or sometimes geared to candidates with special needs, eg, large print for candidates with limited vision.

Even when candidates seem to understand the APL process, some advisors find it useful to summarise or review the process just to be sure the candidate has no questions. They also highlight the role of the assessor and make sure the candidate is clear on the differences between 'advising' and 'assessing'. The advisor must make sure candidates realise that he or she is the 'advocate', not the 'gatekeeper' and that at the end of the process, it will be the assessor, not the advisor, who actually does the assessment.

Once the advisor is sure the candidate understands the APL process, it is important to check the candidate's aims, the basic purpose of this stage of the interview. To do this, advisors need to begin the questioning process and listen carefully to the candidate's responses. If the candidate seems to have unrealistic aims and cannot be helped by the APL process, the advisor needs to try to provide other information, if available, that may be more useful to the candidate.

However, if the candidate's aims are likely to be met by the APL process and the benefits to the candidate are quite obvious, the advisor will want to record the agreed aims and move on to stage three of the interview.

Before leaving this stage of the interview, however, it is important to add that most advisors make extensive use of the candidate's application form which in most APL services is completed and sent to the advisor well before the interview begins. The application form can provide basic information about the candidate's work and voluntary experience, his or her reasons for seeking APL and other details that the organisation and the advisors feel will be most useful to all concerned.

Clearly as the advisor and the candidate begin their work together, the advisor should encourage the candidate to ask as many questions as may arise. Similarly, it is the advisor's responsibility to ask questions too to help clarify the candidate's expectations and his or her aims in seeking APL recognition.

Stage 3: Reflecting on the candidate's experience and accomplishments
During this stage the advisor must work with the candidate to

identify those experiences and accomplishments most relevant to the candidate's aims. Again, the application form can provide the basis for many of the questions the advisor will want to ask. The candidate's responses will lead the advisor to ask others.

To encourage candidates' reflections, advisors generally use two types of questions: open- and closed-ended questions.

- An open-ended question requires the candidate to elucidate or develop his or her thoughts. For example, if the advisor said, 'I notice from your application form that you have had several different jobs in computing over the past five years', and then asked, 'What did you like or dislike about each one?', that would be an open-ended question. The candidate could respond and elaborate as he or she felt necessary.
- A closed-ended question requires the candidate to give a specific response. For example, if the advisor said, 'I notice from your application form that you also worked in the local hotel. Did you supervise staff there too?', then the candidate would be required to answer 'yes' or 'no'.

Examples of other open-ended questions include:

- How did you feel about that?
- Sounds interesting . . . tell me more . . . .
- Why did you decide to do that?

Examples of other closed-ended questions include:

- Did you use power tools?
- How often did you do that?
- How long ago did you complete that qualification?

Candidates will vary considerably in their ability to reflect and express themselves with the advisor. Advisors will generally find it necessary to use a wide variety of open- and closed-ended questions to help candidates develop their profiles. During this phase, it is essential that the advisor demonstrates good active listening skills so that each candidate is encouraged throughout the process. In summary, at this stage advisors will find that they need to:

- elicit information from the candidate, both general and specific;
- provide ongoing feedback;
- point out associations and linkages whenever possible; and
- help the candidate integrate or mould his or her reflections into a coherent profile.

Stage 4: Linking the candidate profile to the recognition or qualifications sought

This stage is essentially an extension of stage 3, during which candidates link their profiles to the qualifications or units of recognition on offer. Once the candidate and advisor agree the general direction in which the candidate wishes to go, the advisor must provide information about the various qualifications (or units) on offer that seem consistent with the candidate's personal aims and his or her objectives in seeking APL.

Candidates might begin by looking at the titles of qualifications or units in the areas of interest and from these select those that best reflect their accomplishments and competence. In higher education contexts candidates may need to see the descriptions or learning outcomes for the courses for which they are hoping to receive accreditation. Those in further education in the UK might review the NVQs in their areas.

It is important during this stage that the candidate receive as much support and help as possible. Advisors need to encourage the candidate's active involvement in linking his or her profile to the units or qualifications on offer. This is not always an easy activity for candidates to undertake. Often they are unsure of the standards of performance expected or of the language being used. The advisor should try to guide the candidate without being prescriptive.

Many organisations develop checklists to help candidates

through this process. The checklists should reflect in easy-to-understand language the standards, learning outcomes or courses on offer and can be offered in either paper and pencil or computer format.

Advisors must make sure that candidates have adequate time to complete this stage of the work. Sometimes candidates will want to take the checklists home to complete before resuming the interview with the advisor on another day. The main outcome of this stage of the interview is the identification of the qualifications or units for which the candidate wishes to be assessed and receive accreditation.

Stage 5: Matching specific skills and knowledge to the standards or learning outcomes specified in the qualification
During this stage candidates must complete two different activities:

1. They must begin to match their specific skills and knowledge to the requirements specified in the qualifications, units or courses for which they are seeking credit.
2. They must begin to identify possible sources of evidence that they can use to prove that they really do possess the skills and knowledge they claim.

Both of these steps require that the candidate take a closer look at the specifications on offer and receive information on the nature of acceptable evidence that could be used.

Once again, many advisors find it most helpful to use checklists at this point in the process. As in stage 3, candidates may wish to:

- complete the checklists with the advisor;
- complete the checklists in a nearby room, after making a start with the advisor;
- take the checklists home to complete; or
- use a computer data bank of checklists.

Advisors need to be prepared to describe to candidates the nature of acceptable evidence that might be used in the candidate's portfolio so that, as they complete the checklists, they can begin to make notes regarding the evidence they have available, could acquire or generate. Once completed, these checklists serve as the basis for the candidate's final claims to credit.

Before moving on to stage 6, it is important to highlight the iterative nature of stages 3, 4 and 5. For any given candidate, these three stages may overlap or candidates may need to go back and forth between stages. For example, it is not unusual for a candidate to continue to add to or modify his or her profile (stage 3) as he or she works with the checklists presented in stages 4 and 5. Very often the checklists will suggest activities, accomplishments or skills that the candidate may have forgotten or dismissed as unimportant. Similarly, candidates frequently come to see that they know and can do a lot more than they originally thought and therefore often change their aims (or the qualifications) they are seeking.

Advisors need to be sensitive to the needs of each candidate and be willing to adapt the interview accordingly. Candidates progress through these three stages of the interview at their own rate and in their own manner. Some may have a very clear idea of how to work with checklists and compare themselves to the standards; others will need a lot of support. By using a staged interview approach, advisors will have a clear notion of the outcomes each candidate needs to achieve and a framework in which to offer the necessary help and support.

Stage 6: Developing an action or assessment plan
This final stage of the interview brings the candidate and the advisor to a point of agreement about the work to follow. It allows the candidate the opportunity to commit to paper his or her plan to continue with the APL process. It also provides the advisor with a document by which he or she can support and encourage the candidate.

An action or assessment plan is a simple form completed by

the candidate and signed by the advisor that specifies what the candidate intends to do next. It specifies:

- the qualification, units or learning outcomes for which the candidate is seeking credit;
- possible sources of evidence; and
- a date for the submission of the portfolio or a date by which the candidate will be ready for assessment.

In some cases, candidates need to enrol in a programme before receiving further access to the advisor or group support. In others, candidates need to indicate exactly when and how they plan to collect or generate their evidence *and* progress with new learning. The action or assessment plan is signed and dated by both the advisor and the candidate and each retains a copy.

This final stage of the staged interview is the same for candidates seeking APL through an educational or training provider. The terminology and the time-scale may vary, but all effective APL services need to develop a comparable action-oriented framework.

Variations on the interview
As with all staged or structured interviews, there are any number of variations possible. In the one just described, for example, there are some APL programmes which rely much more on the candidates' self-assessment to encourage reflection and to link their strengths to qualifications and standards or learning outcomes on offer. Working with either workbooks, checklists or some other form of stimulation, a candidate may not need to meet with his or her advisor except to review and finalise the action or assessment plan.

Similarly, in some employment contexts it is possible for people to work in small groups to develop their profiles and identify their aims, strengths and sources of evidence. In this case the advisor may serve as facilitator to the group, meeting with individual candidates only at the end of the process to sign the action or assessment plan. In still other APL models, the staged interview may need to take place over several pre-defined sessions.

Materials needed*

As was stated earlier, APL requires significant monitoring and record-keeping. It is not surprising, therefore, that it often requires a lot of paperwork. A complete and accessible file needs to be maintained for each candidate. Many people – assessors, registrars, quality assurance personnel, the candidates themselves – will need to use the file, so it is important that the documentation is as clear, accurate and up-to-date as possible. What follows is a list and brief description of the forms that might be used to monitor a candidate's progress through the APL process.

1. *Checklist of interview stages*

Many advisors find it useful to create a document by which they can monitor the progress of each candidate during the interview itself. They can note the outcomes of each phase and record actions to be taken by the candidate and/or themselves. Such checklists can also provide useful feedback information to the candidates. As other forms and documents are completed and placed in the candidate's file, this checklist can be discarded.

2. *Application form*

All APL services require candidates to complete some sort of application form which is generally sent to the organisation before the candidate comes for the interview. The application form should be user-friendly with large enough print for the candidates to be able to read the directions and adequate space provided for them to enter their responses. (Many adults complain that the forms used for traditional-aged students are very difficult to see.)

The information requested on the application form will vary from one organisation to another. But essentially, it should

* This section has been adapted from OU (1990) *APL: An Open Learning Pack for Advisors and Assessors.*

collect brief information about the candidate's current and past activities and request a statement of why the candidate is seeking APL.

Some candidates may have difficulty completing the form on their own because of a literacy problem or physical disability. If this is the case, the providing organisation will need to provide the assistance these candidates need. (This is true, of course, for all the other forms and documents candidates may need to complete.)

3. *Qualifications on offer*

Each candidate will need to review a list of the qualifications or programmes on offer for which he or she could seek accreditation of prior learning. In some organisations, such as a college, which has an institutional commitment to offer APL across all its qualifications and programmes, this presents no major problem. However, some organisations only offer APL for a portion of their offerings. Both advisors and candidates need to know what these offerings are.

Even with the best of lists, many candidates will need further explanations about the qualifications or programmes being offered. Although many advisors are used to working with the language (and jargon!), most candidates are not. Advisors should therefore be prepared to answer questions in clear, jargon-free language.

4. *Checklists of standards or learning outcomes*

All candidates will need to know what is expected of them. They need to be able to equate what they know and can do with what is on offer at the APL centre. One way for centres to help candidates do this is to develop checklists based on the standards or learning outcomes related to each of the qualifications on offer. Usually it is the assessors or the subject specialists who develop these checklists in consultation with the advisors. Sometimes APL services also provide guidelines to candidates on how to complete the checklists and offer examples of completed checklists (with sources of evidence noted) for candidates to review.

5. *Action or assessment plan*

These plans serve as a type of contract between the candidate and the providing organisation. The main purpose of the plan is to:

1. spell out the qualifications or units the candidate is claiming;
2. indicate types of evidence the candidate will be gathering or generating;
3. indicate the time frame in which the portfolio or assessment is to be completed; and
4. provide a space for both the candidate and the advisor to sign and date the agreement or plan.

6. *Guide to portfolio production*

At the end of the interview, most candidates will begin to gather and/or generate the needed evidence to support their claims to credit. Since this evidence is most often put into some sort of binder, candidates need to receive a guide that describes the desired structure of the portfolio, the forms needed, and examples of acceptable evidence. In general, the better the portfolio guidance, the more likely that candidates will submit stronger, better organised portfolios.

7. *Guide to services*

Candidates also need to know what other services are on offer. Are there portfolio development workshops, peer support groups, a video in the library they can refer to or open workshops in which they can develop new skills and knowledge or competence? APL centres should be prepared to develop some sort of guide to services or a candidate resource handbook.

Portfolio production

Following the interview, candidates need to gather or generate their evidence in order to construct their portfolios. During this period which can last from a matter or weeks to several months, advisors need to be able to provide a range of support. They need to:

- provide information;
- respond to questions;
- review the candidates' work;
- encourage candidates;
- liaise with assessors; and
- give candidates fair and accurate feedback.

They also need to review finished portfolios for completeness, readability and organisation. It is not for the advisor to act as assessor, that is, to determine whether the candidate fully satisfies the specified requirements, but it is the advisor's job to help the candidate present him or herself in the best possible light. Advisors must guard against doing the candidate's job. One of the strengths of the APL process is that the onus of responsibility is on the candidate. Advisors are there to offer a helping hand; but it is the candidate who must do the work.

Adult development issues

Many people who become APL advisors or assessors find themselves working with adults for the first time. They are often quite surprised to experience how different it is to work with adults rather than with traditional-aged students. Adults are often more focused and more aware of their own goals. They may be balancing all the adult roles of partner, parent, worker, and community volunteer and feel they have very little time left for themselves. APL, with its flexibility and self-direction components often is a way by which adults can find a bit of time to focus on their own needs. It is therefore essential that they make the best use of the time available to them to progress through the APL process. As we have already noted, they will look to the providing institution to provide support, minimise red tape, and actively help them reach their goals.

Many professionals new to APL find it useful to read some of the background literature about adult development and adult-learning issues. They find that it helps them to understand not only more about the people they find themselves working with but also about themselves, as professional and as adult learners.

There is a growing body of excellent literature emerging in this field and no doubt most college and university libraries will provide ample reading material for the interested reader. However, a few of the more pioneering thinkers may provide a useful starting point for additional investigation; a list is given at the end of this chapter.

Summary

The role of the advisor in APL is primarily one of supporting and mentoring candidates through the APL process. To do this effectively, it is necessary for the advisor to demonstrate a range of skills. They need to be able to work *with* candidates rather than *for* candidates in helping them reflect on their skills and accomplishments.

The advisor has to be prepared to work with a wide range of candidates. Candidates will vary considerably in terms of their skills and accomplishments as well as in terms of their motivation and commitment to the APL programme. The advisor must be flexible enough to work with all candidates in the most appropriate manner: empowering and stimulating interest in those who lack self confidence, whilst providing facts and figures for others.

Advisors also need to be able to offer specific guidance and advice for candidates when they are gathering evidence for their portfolio. However, throughout the process, it is the candidates themselves who must assume responsibility for portfolio production not their advisors. Advisors need to be good listeners to respond fully to candidates' varied needs in the most sensitive and effective way possible.

Further reading

Cross, K P (1981) *Adults as Learners: Increasing Participation and Facilitating Learning*, Jossey-Bass, San Francisco.

Cross, K P (1986) *Adults as Learners*, Jossey-Bass, San Francisco.

Gould, R (1978) *Transformations: Growth and Change in Adult Life*, Simon & Schuster, New York.

Knowles, M S (1970) *The Modern Practice of Adult Education: Andragogy Versus Pedagogy*, Association Press, New York.

Kolb, D A (1976) *Learning Styles Inventory: Technical Manual*, McBer and Company, Boston.

Levinson, D, Darrow, C N Klein, E G, Levinson, M H and McKee, B (1978) *The Seasons of a Man's Life*, Knopf, New York.

Chapter 4

Providing for Groups

Introduction

Although advisors can and do provide significant support to candidates individually, increasingly institutions offering APL are introducing group activities to assist candidates. The reasons for this are many. First, many organisations have found that providing the one-to-one support described in the last chapter can be potentially expensive. They have come to realise that providing services to groups of candidates can significantly reduce the time required of any particular advisor. They also have found that although some candidates most assuredly require considerable support individually, some do not and that those who can, are quite satisfied to work with less extensive one-to-one support.

Second, some candidates actually prefer *not* to work individually with an advisor; they prefer the familiarity of working with other adults like themselves who are aiming for a common goal. They are happy to progress at their own pace with a variety of written materials, peer support and an occasional conversation with the advisor.

Third, many professionals who provide APL advice and support have expressed concern that adults choosing to acquire qualifications through APL rather than through more traditional means may lose out on vital learning interactions that often occur during traditional educational and training instruction. They believe that when people work together there is an important learning experience that occurs which enhances the development of each individual. APL advisors have also reported that candidates working in groups often avoid the feelings of isolation sometimes expressed by those candidates who do not have group support options.

For all of these reasons and no doubt others, colleges, universities, employers and others who offer APL are developing a variety of ways to work with groups. This chapter will review in detail some of the options open to professionals wishing to develop a number of group activities as part of their APL service.

APL briefing sessions

One of the most popular ways of introducing potential candidates to APL is through a briefing session. Whether one hour or three, these briefing sessions often serve to introduce potential candidates to the APL process for the first time. They allow potential candidates to meet others like themselves and to ask questions about the APL process and the likely outcomes. Many briefing sessions also offer an opportunity for potential candidates to begin the self-assessment and reflection process so vital in APL.

The briefing session occurs at the pre-entry stage. Its primary purpose is to increase potential candidates' awareness of the APL process, describe its value and in general help individuals decide whether or not they wish to embark on the APL route.

An effective briefing session must provide information, facilitate communication and enable individuals to have their questions answered. It should be well organised and delivered in an interesting, friendly manner.

Usually advisors deliver the APL briefing sessions and most often they use a variety of techniques to illustrate their points, disseminate information, facilitate discussion, and encourage feedback and questions from the participants. To no small extent it is the advisor's presentation and listening skills that will determine the effectiveness of the session.

Briefing session participants

Before an advisor can effectively plan for the briefing session, he or she must be clear about who the participants will be. The advisor responsible for the briefing session will want to know well in advance who is likely to attend and what their primary purposes are in seeking recognition for their prior learning.

Often, briefing sessions are open to any interested adult. Others may be designed for homogeneous groups, for example, managers from a particular company or other occupationally-specific groups. Still others may be organised around the needs of a particular community group. Although the basic information the advisor will want to convey is the same, the tone, examples, and responses to particular questions may differ considerably.

The level of literacy skills of the potential candidates may be another important factor which influences the content and manner of the briefing session. Clearly if the potential candidates have limited reading ability, advisors will need to rely more on oral communication than written. They also may find that people with reading problems lack self-confidence in other areas of their lives. The advisor may therefore need to plan different types of activities or group discussions to encourage the development of people's self-confidence.

Similarly, there may be people within any potential candidate group who have special needs. Every effort should be made to provide for these individuals too, whether that means ensuring that the venue can be accessed by wheelchair or that large-print versions of some materials are available. Often very small modifications in a given programme or venue can make all the difference to people with special needs. If a potential client group speaks English as a second language, some materials might also be offered in the participants' own language.

The briefing session venue

Potential candidates may come to the briefing session quite nervous. Every effort should be made to welcome them and make sure they are comfortable. The briefing session should be held in a well-lit, well-ventilated room that is easily accessible and clean. There should be adequate public transport or parking with clear directions provided to candidates well in advance of the session.

Most briefing session rooms should be large enough to accommodate the full group – perhaps up to 25 people – but be small enough so that people can be encouraged to speak in small groups. If possible, tables with five or six chairs often work well for the group discussions. Toilets should be near the room and of course ramps or other facilities provided for people with disabilities.

Time of day and length of session

Briefing sessions should be held on days and at times convenient to the participants. If the participants are employed, for example, the session might be held in the evening or on Saturday. If the session is intended for people who are primarily unemployed, the session might be conveniently organised during the day. Alternatively, if the session is to be held on the premises of a particular employer, then the employer will in all likelihood identify the best time of day to hold the session. There is no single best time to hold a briefing session: the best time is one that is convenient to the participants and the convener.

The length of an APL briefing session will depend on a number of factors, not the least of which are the expected outcomes of the session. Most briefing sessions are held for two to four hours. Longer sessions are sometimes organised, but these usually include additional purposes, eg they provide ample opportunity for self-assessment for individuals' personal career development.

Most advisors find that with experience they are flexible

enough to offer briefing sessions of varying lengths, depending on the needs of the groups, the context in which the session is being offered and any other factors unique to the particular situation.

Refreshments

As with other training or educational events, the availability of light refreshments – tea, coffee, or fruit juice – often contributes to a more welcoming, friendly atmosphere. Many participants may not have attended an educational or training event for many years; offering them light refreshment is one way to help them relax. People coming from work or other commitments may be especially appreciative. Clearly, though, however desirable it may be to have refreshments available, this is a matter that can only be determined by the local situation and available resources.

Materials and audio-visual aids

At the briefing session, advisors will want to have all the relevant materials they need to conduct the session. Materials might include brochures or leaflets about the APL service, a listing of fees, a schedule of portfolio development workshops, an application form, other learning or training options offered by the centre, etc.

The materials themselves should be informative, readable and easy to use. The briefing session facilitator will want to make sure that all of the materials have a purpose and are relevant to the needs of the participants. It is important to guard against overwhelming participants with too much paper. Often a lot of 'required' reading can discourage people from moving forward with APL.

As with any effective public presentation, the use of interesting audio-visual materials can serve to enhance the communication of the facilitator and increase the understanding of the participants. Key points about APL, the services of the centre, and the process candidates undergo can all be well illustrated on slides, overhead transparencies or a video.

Clearly each facilitator needs to use materials and techniques with which he or she feels comfortable. But as has been emphasised elsewhere in this book, different people have different ways of learning things and may respond more or less positively to any one. For that reason, it is often a good idea for advisors to develop more than one way to convey the messages delivered during the briefing session.

A *team approach*

Most APL advisors learn to conduct different types of briefing sessions. Depending on the context in which they are working, the number of people expected at the session, the resources available and other factors, some centres take a team approach in delivering APL briefing sessions.

Sometimes two advisors work together; sometimes an assessor contributes to an advisor's presentation. In some centres successful candidates are also invited to provide a brief input and respond to participants' questions. Many other options are possible, of course. It is up to each centre to determine the most appropriate people to deliver the APL briefing session.

If more than one person is delivering separate briefing sessions, however, it is important for the centre to make sure that staff are doing so in a comparable way and do not contradict each other. If the content, time frame, activities and materials are developed by the team of people who are to deliver the session, there is greater likelihood that participants will have similar, if not identical, briefing session experiences. Regular reviews and evaluations of the briefing sessions should be undertaken, and systematic evaluation feedback collected from all participants.

Content of the briefing session

The exact content of a briefing session will vary from one context to another and depend on a number of other factors already cited. However, almost all follow a similar basic framework that includes:

- welcome and introductions;
- the purpose of the session;
- an overview of the purpose and process of APL;
- an introduction to the standards, learning outcomes, courses or programmes for which APL is available;
- an introduction to the nature of evidence;
- a question and answer period; and
- a closing session.

Most briefing sessions include some sort of ice-breaker at the beginning of the programme and an opportunity for each member of the group to tell something about him or herself. This not only allows the advisor to learn something about each group member, it also begins to foster the early stages of reflection for each participant.

The overview of APL should describe the main benefits of the process, the steps needed to be taken, and the roles of the key people. It should also describe the separate responsibilities of the advisor, assessor and the candidate during each of the stages and provide a clear idea of the range of support services offered by the centre.

To fully understand the APL process and the benefits to be gained, each participant will need an opportunity to consider the standards, learning outcomes and/or qualifications on offer. Participants might be invited to complete mini check-lists of competences they might be claiming or discuss in structured small group discussions their accomplishments or areas of strength.

The concept of evidence is best introduced by giving participants an opportunity to see one or more examples of portfolios and/or generating their own lists of evidence in a structured group activity led by the advisor. Even at this early stage, advisors should help the participants understand the breadth of acceptable evidence and some of the criteria by which assessors will judge it.

Throughout the session, the facilitator(s) should encourage the prospective candidates to ask questions and identify areas of concern. The facilitator will also want to provide a clear picture of the various steps people can take as a result of attending the session:

1. To begin the APL process.
2. To embark on another option within the centre.
3. To consider the options, and make a decision later on.

The closing session should thank people for coming and provide an opportunity for the potential candidates to ask any further questions.

Portfolio development workshops

The portfolio development workshop is another effective way of working with candidates in groups. Unlike the briefing session which is for *potential* candidates, the portfolio development workshop is intended to support people already committed to the APL process. These workshops are generally offered during stage three of the process, gathering evidence.

There are several basic purposes served by portfolio development workshops. These include:

- motivating the candidate to analyse his/her past accomplishments and current competence;
- helping the candidate to select or develop the most appropriate evidence for his/her portfolio;
- helping the candidate construct his/her portfolio; and
- preparing the candidate for assessment.

Research has shown that candidates who make use of the portfolio development workshop and go on to complete the

APL process, do so with increased self-confidence, heightened self-awareness, and a greater ability to organise and integrate information (Warren and Breen, 1976; Hall, 1991).

The design

Portfolio development workshops can be designed in many different ways and can be offered for different periods of time.

Some APL centres run portfolio development workshops on an open basis so that candidates can drop in and out over several months, depending on their needs. A single facilitator or advisor is present to respond to questions, organise small group discussions and otherwise serve as a resource to the candidates who show up.

Other centres provide a more structured approach with each of several sessions focusing on particular points or issues. Generally, these sessions are also facilitated by a single advisor, although sometimes assessors are invited to discuss with the group particular issues relating to the acceptability of the evidence.

Still other centres, most often colleges and universities, offer portfolio development courses for credit in and of themselves, regardless of the outcomes of the assessment of the candidates' portfolios. In these cases the course is usually organised around a particular theme such as the development of academic or vocational skills, personal or career development, the meaning of education, careers orientation, etc (Michelson and Mandell 1988). In this model, candidates produce their portfolios as an outcome of the course.

Lastly, some APL centres offer periodic portfolio development workshops, often only three to four hours in length. This single session is designed to cover two basic topics: acceptable evidence and the construction of the portfolio. These sessions are usually intended to supplement other written materials and are offered primarily to motivate and provide candidates with more concrete hands-on information about portfolio development.

Many of the points made about briefing sessions are applicable, of course, to portfolio development workshops as well: the need for an appropriate venue, the desirability of refreshments, the use of clear and relevant materials and audio-visual aids, etc. What follows is a detailed description of the essential content of portfolio development workshops which will be applicable to most candidates' needs, regardless of the type of workshop offered or its duration. Variations can be developed based on the additional needs of the candidates, the requirements of the providing organisations or options developed by the advisors offering the workshops.

It is important to add that the content of the portfolio development workshop can also be used to advise and support candidates in one-on-one situations.

The content

The content of portfolio development workshops generally falls into four categories:

1. understanding the standards;
2. defining the nature of acceptable evidence;
3. constructing the portfolio; and
4. preparing for assessment.

We will look at each of these in detail.

Understanding the standards

Portfolio development workshops provide an excellent forum in which candidates can come to understand and use the standards. Candidates are better able to develop their evidence and prepare for assessment when they understand the standards or learning outcomes on offer.

Using the standards in the portfolio development workshop also allows candidates to continue the reflection and iterative process of APL. By working with the standards, reflecting on their own understanding of them, candidates often come to see their achievements in a new light. Things they may have forgotten are remembered; experiences that once seemed random suddenly fall into place as part of a previously unperceived learning pattern.

Advisors, working with assessors, in advance of the portfolio development workshops, need to make sure that candidates have access to all the information necessary to use and understand the standards. Examples of previously prepared portfolios or particular experiences of other candidates can be particularly helpful.

Evidence
The concept of evidence actually stems from the notion of assessment. In the context of the emerging NVQs described in the first chapter, the Employment Department, the National Council for Vocational Qualifications and others in Britain define assessment as:

> The gathering and interpretation of evidence based on the candidates' performance as judged against the standards (elements of competence and performance criteria). The purpose of assessment is to confirm when candidates are competent and entitled to accreditation.

All assessment requires evidence. It is important for advisors and candidates alike to understand the basic concept of evidence. Whether we make an informal assessment, eg, 'It's raining, therefore I need my umbrella', or a more formal one, eg, 'This job applicant seems to meet my requirements and has presented very strong letters of recommendation', we are using evidence to make our assessments.

In the first example, we have *observed* the rain (gathered direct evidence) and this has helped us to make the decision to carry an umbrella. In the second example, we have probably interviewed the candidate (gathered direct evidence) and have reviewed letters about the candidate (gathered indirect evidence) before making the decision about whether or not to hire the applicant. Throughout our lives we use evidence in this way, no matter how small or large or how formal or informal our decision-making process.

One of the first principles, then, in introducing APL candidates to the idea of evidence is to convey that they have been collecting evidence and making decisions based on that evidence since they were babies. The concept of evidence should not be new to anyone. It should be seen as a natural, everyday phenomenon.

It is also useful to help candidates think of the many ways they previously have been assessed either during their formal education or in employment: they may have produced reports, completed special projects, taken written examinations, participated in classroom discussions – all of these activities are methods by which teachers and supervisors routinely gather evidence to make grading, ranking or pay award decisions.

Once candidates have a clear idea of the nature of evidence, it is important to move on to let them know what is different about APL evidence, namely that in APL the assessment process – and therefore the evidence – is not linked to any *particular* learning or training programme. It is therefore the candidate's responsibility to gather or generate the evidence that will match the standards or learning outcomes set by the providing institution. Unlike most traditional assessment, APL candidates actually have a great deal of control over the evidence used in their assessment. Most professional trainers and educators spend a great deal of time devising ways to assess their traditional students or trainees. In APL, once the standards or learning outcomes are in place, it is the candidates who must generate as much suitable evidence as they can to prove their competence against the standards.

Two types of evidence are used in the APL process: direct evidence and indirect evidence. Direct evidence refers to something the candidate produces him or herself. Examples may include:

- a computer program;
- a training manual;
- a musical composition;
- a magazine article;
- a budget forecast;
- a video production and so forth.

Examples of indirect evidence may include:

- letters from past or current employers;
- special awards or certificates;
- newspaper articles about the candidate;
- photographs of other work produced by the candidate and so forth.

Generally direct evidence is considered stronger than indirect evidence but both are useful to candidates as they develop their portfolios. Portfolio development workshops need to provide ample opportunities for candidates to identify and explore these two types of evidence.

In constructing their portfolios, candidates will need to use a combination of direct and indirect evidence to support their claims to credit. For example, one manager seeking recognition of her competence to monitor and control the use of resources presented the following evidence:

1. A proposal relating to improvements she had devised (direct).
2. Memos detailing the outcomes of several meetings she had had with her line manager and others within her organisation (indirect).
3. Annual financial reports, showing cost savings in her areas of responsibility (indirect).
4. A personal report, prepared by the candidate, describing the problem she faced, the alternatives available to her and her organisation, her decision-making process and a verbal summary of the outcomes (direct).

Another candidate seeking accreditation for a unit in engineering brought in several components he had produced (direct) and letters from his previous and current employers (indirect), each of which described his work and verified that he had produced those components. Evidence need not always be paper!

During the portfolio development workshop, candidates should be encouraged to collect or generate the strongest evidence they can. However, in so doing the workshop needs to introduce and highlight two important factors related to the evidence: authenticity and currency.

1. *Authenticity*: Assessors will want to ensure that the work submitted by the candidate really is the result of his or her own effort. There are many ways that candidates can provide evidence of the authenticity of their work. They can present letters from others to substantiate their evidence; they can submit additional corroborative evidence; they can prepare a substantiated narrative statement; or they can be prepared to answer questions posed by the assessor about the evidence.

Sometimes if candidates have been part of a team effort, the issue of authenticity presents unique problems for both the candidate and the assessor. In this case, candidates usually must provide one or more additional pieces of evidence which clearly attest to the candidate's own accomplishments or contributions to the group's work.

2. *Currency*: The concept of currency relates to how recent the evidence is. In most cases candidates will need to be given clear guidelines regarding this matter. For example, in the area of information technology, evidence more than one or two years old might be deemed too old and therefore inappropriate. On the other hand, a writer or journalist may well be able to submit evidence one or two years old, assuming it was relevant to the standards or learning outcomes in place.

During the portfolio development workshops, candidates need to be given the opportunity to work with the concepts of authenticity and currency to make sure they can accurately apply them to the preparation of their own portfolios.

Selecting evidence

To help individuals select their evidence, the advisor needs to assist candidates during the portfolio development workshop to focus on the *outcomes* of their learning. There is a great tendency among adults to want to provide information about the *process* of learning something. If clear standards or learning outcomes are in place, however, the emphasis must be on the products of the candidate's achievements. This is not always an easy task, particularly since the outcomes of a candidate's performance may not yield concrete evidence.

For example, consider a probation officer who lacks a formal qualification but who has been performing his job competently for a number of years. One of his main responsibilities may be to support offenders during the period of probation. The officer may meet with a particular offender on a regular basis, provide information, guidance and advice and still the offender may break his or her probation restrictions. Does this mean that the probation officer has not done a good job and would not have evidence of his competence as a probation officer if he were to seek APL to gain a formal qualification?

In this example, as with many other helping or service occupations it is indeed a range of processes for which the candidate must show evidence. Hopefully, these processes would be spelled out clearly in the standards. For example, responsibilities of a probation officer might be to:
Assist clients to make use of available services and information.
(Care Sector Consortium, 1990)

To do this, the standards might further specify that the probation officer should be able to:
Assist the client to access services and facilities, and
Encourage the client to use services and facilities.

The APL candidate would therefore be expected to provide evidence that he had assisted and encouraged the client to access and use various services and facilities. There are many ways that this evidence could be provided, through written reports, memos, authenticated interviews, perhaps even a video or audio tape. The fact that the offender broke parole, although an unfortunate outcome, may not be attributable to the probation officer's lack of competence.

So although the focus of APL assessments is on the outcomes of achievements, candidates need to:

1. be directed by the standards, and
2. see that some of the outcomes of their efforts in work or other activities may not provide the most useful or appropriate type of evidence needed.

Many academic and vocational areas lend themselves to product evidence: art, design, composing, computer programing, management, engineering, horticulture – all of these and many other occupational or academic areas are based on product evidence. Candidates coming from these areas seeking recognition for their prior learning generally have little difficulty in identifying products to help them prove their competence.

Sometimes candidates seek recognition or credit in areas for which they have little or no evidence. For example, a local history buff or someone interested in philosophy may not be able to generate any substantial proof of their learning. In cases such as these, it is up to the advisor to help candidates prepare for other types of assessment – special projects, oral questioning, etc – which are discussed in the next chapter.

In selecting their evidence, candidates also need to think about its relevance. They need to make sure that what they are presenting is directly related to the standards for which they are trying to prove competence. They also need to be reminded that assessors are more interested in the *quality* of the evidence than in the quantity. An abundance of evidence may actually undermine a candidate's claim if it is not relevant to the learning outcomes or standards on offer or is not of sufficient breadth or diversity.

Letters of validation

Special mention must be made about letters of validation. These are useful sources of indirect evidence that many candidates include in their portfolios. During portfolio development workshops, candidates need to receive information on how to request these letters and how to make sure they obtain the type of information they need from the letter writer.

First and foremost it is essential that candidates remember that it is their own responsibility to obtain the letters of validation they need, not the APL centre's or the advisor's. Candidates must carefully consider who they might approach to request a letter of validation. It need not be a current supervisor. Many candidates request letters of validation from previous supervisors, clients or colleagues. They may also request them of people who know of their work outside the work environment. For example, people in the voluntary sector may be able to obtain a letter from a regional director, or from the accountant, bank manager, public relations officer – anyone who is familiar with the candidate's work and is willing to write on his or her behalf.

To request a letter of validation, candidates will need to:

1. specify the purpose of the letter and the date by which the candidate needs the letter;
2. spell out the competences or learning outcomes for which he or she is seeking recognition or accreditation (explicit standards are very helpful here);
3. provide the name and address of the person to whom the letter should be sent; and
4. as a courtesy include a stamped, properly addressed envelope.

The candidate should also plan to thank the letter writer in advance and provide information on how he or she can be reached should the letter writer have questions.

Most letters of validation are sent to the APL advisor who then passes them on to the candidate for inclusion in the portfolio. However, some letter writers prefer to send the letters directly to candidates.

Many APL centres provide a prototype of a letter to help candidates develop their own letters of validation and in some cases centres also provide written guidelines for the letter writers themselves. An example of a letter, which has been adapted from material produced by the Open University (OU, 1990) is shown in Figure 4.1.

During the portfolio development workshop, candidates should be given an opportunity to develop their letters of validation and/or request clarification about their preparation from the advisor.

Constructing the portfolio

The portfolio development workshop also needs to provide candidates with clear instructions and guidance on the construction of their portfolios. The better organised a portfolio is, the easier it is to assess. For this reason, APL centres are encouraged to provide specific guidelines on the construction of portfolios.

While any number of options are possible, experience suggests that the most readable portfolios contain the following sections:

1. A cover which contains the name, address and day-time phone number of the candidate. The purpose of the cover is to identify the candidate at a glance and to provide easy access to his or her contact telephone number.
2. A table of contents listing each section and its starting page number. As in all written material, a table of contents offers the reader a clear map to the contents of the document.
3. A narrative statement, completed checklist or detailed C.V. which relates the candidate's competences to the standards, units or learning outcomes being claimed. The purpose of this section is to show a clear relationship between what the candidate did and what he or she is

Dear _____ ,

Thank you for agreeing to write a letter of validation on behalf of an accreditation of prior learning (APL) candidate from this centre. As you are no doubt aware, APL is a process by which individuals are able to receive recognition and accreditation for skills they have learned in a variety of ways. Your letter will help the centre determine whether or not the candidate has attained the competences he or she has claimed. While your letter may play a critical role in the candidate's assessment, it may not be used as the sole source of information. Usually APL candidates are assessed in a variety of ways.

To be most helpful, your letter should be typed on company or business notepaper and contain the following:

– the candidate's name;
– the date(s) of his or her employment or association with you;
– the post(s) held by the candidate or a description of the capacity in which you know/knew him or her;
– a list of the competences the candidate is claiming and to which you are attesting; and
– your signature and position.

Thank your for your time and assistance in preparing this letter.

Figure 4.1 *A sample candidate letter*

claiming. Many assessors find that when they review the evidence in a portfolio, they have difficulty understanding the context in which the evidence was produced. Increasingly, therefore, candidates are being asked to provide sufficient detail about their background, the competences they are claiming and the evidence they are submitting to help the assessors understand exactly what they have accomplished as represented by the evidence in the portfolio.

4. A cross-reference system relating the evidence to the units, elements of competence or learning outcomes being claimed. Again, candidates need to provide clear guidance in their portfolios so that the assessors can easily consider the evidence in relation to the particular units or learning outcomes being claimed. Since some pieces of evidence may support the claim for more than one unit or learning outcome, candidates need to show the assessor exactly what their intention is for each piece of evidence.

5. The evidence itself. Each piece of evidence needs to be clearly labelled to avoid confusion and to make sure the assessor can easily identify the reason it has been included in the portfolio.

During the portfolio development workshop, candidates will need to review each of these sections, receive whatever guidance the centre normally provides, and have a chance to ask questions about each section. In many portfolio development workshops, candidates are given an opportunity to develop their narrative statements and receive feedback from their peers and/or the advisor.

Preparation of the portfolio
'Neatness counts' is an old adage that still holds true. In preparing their portfolios candidates need to be reminded to use standard English, to make sure they amend spelling and grammatical errors and that they organise their work clearly and effectively. Although most assessors will not be assessing the language or organisation *per se*, the readability of the portfolio is important. If assessors find themselves struggling to understand what a candidate has included in his or her portfolio, they will often be dismissive of the evidence itself. The message from assessors is clear: candidates should take care to present their portfolios as neatly and clearly as possible.

Preparing for assessment

Portfolio development workshops must also help candidates to prepare for assessment. Candidates should have a clear idea of what will happen to their portfolios once they are complete and know what the assessor will be looking for during his or her review of the evidence. Advisors must be prepared to respond to a wide range of questions on this topic since most candidates, with good reason, want to know what will happen to their work.

As time allows, advisors will want to introduce candidates to the various methods of assessment as described in the next chapter and provide role play or simulation opportunities for the candidates to develop an idea of what each method of assessment is like. It cannot be over-stated that many adults hold deep-seated fears of being tested or assessed. Often they have a keen sense of anxiety or even failure from their earlier days as students. The portfolio development workshop should encourage candidates to see that they have significant control of the assessment process during APL and that they have an opportunity to work *with* the assessor, not just respond *to* his or her requests.

Portfolio development workshops also offer candidates an opportunity to see the purpose behind assessment. So often in traditional assessment situations, the person being assessed sees little reason beyond a grade or score for being evaluated. It is hoped that during the portfolio development workshop, candidates will come to see the reasons for the assessment and the contribution they can make to its success.

Approaches to portfolio development workshops

Portfolio development workshops can provide an exciting opportunity for adults to develop not just their portfolios but themselves. The workshops can offer a focus for reflection unknown to most of us. They can also provide a structured environment in which the candidates have time to consider properly and organise their evidence. Although many people can work on their own, the portfolio development workshop provides a valuable opportunity for both the candidates and their advisors.

Most portfolio development workshops include a great deal of small group work. A certain amount of guidance and input is required of the advisor or facilitator but the real learning opportunities often take place in small group discussions or when candidates receive feedback from one or more members of the workshop or when common problems are tackled by the group.

Organisers of the portfolio development workshops need to make sure that there is ample time for candidates to draw on the resources of the group and to voice their own opinions and issues. In some APL programmes, portfolio development workshops are combined with peer-support groups. These groups meet on an informal basis to help one another in the development of their portfolios. Since no advisor or facilitator is required, these groups can be an efficient and cost-effective way of encouraging candidates to help themselves.

Summary

Group activities are increasingly being used by institutions to support candidates through the APL process. Staff at these institutions recognise that group activities can be more cost-effective than one-to-one advice and that they provide a useful framework for many adults. Experience at a wide range of centres indicates that candidates themselves often prefer working with peers to share their mutual experiences and address common problems. Advisors also recognise that group work helps reduce some candidates' feelings of isolation, stimulates valuable interactions and motivates candidates to complete the APL process.

There are a number of group-based activities professionals use to deliver APL. The initial briefing session is one which allows people to learn about APL and ask questions before they decide whether or not to proceed.

Portfolio development workshops provide another opportunity to work with groups. Candidates can analyse their experiences, identify appropriate evidence, develop their portfolios and prepare for assessment. In portfolio development workshops an advisor can explain to a group of candidates essential information about selecting and gathering evidence, preparing letters of validation, constructing portfolios, preparing for assessment and so forth. To do this on an individual basis would obviously require more time and does not allow for valuable sharing of experiences by the participating candidates.

Chapter 5

Assessment and Quality Assurance

Assessment takes place during the fourth stage of the APL process. It is the critical activity upon which the entire system rests. To no small degree, the credibility of APL depends almost exclusively on the validity, reliability and fairness of the assessment process. For this reason it is essential that professionals planning to establish an APL service learn about and adhere to principles of good practice in assessment.

Principles of good practice

Just what are these principles of good practice? For the purposes of APL, they include a range of technical requirements *and* a range of effective communication skills. In this chapter we look at both.

To begin, APL assessments do not require highly specialised training or skills in test design and statistics. APL assessment requires assessors who are familiar with their fields, the standards that relate to the occupation or area of study to be assessed, and are reasonably effective communicators (Docking, 1990a). APL assessments, like all others, require the assessor to draw inferences from the evidence gathered and presented about the candidate's performance. It requires the assessor to go through a systematic process that will satisfy the candidate, the advisor, other assessors and perhaps external verifiers that the

99

assessment and the resulting decisions were made as validly, reliably and fairly as possible.

Teachers and trainers regularly administer tests and other assessment instruments. These include paper and pencil examinations developed by the teacher; norm-referenced examinations developed and scored by a central body or organisation; special projects; performance-based skills tests; classroom participation; or even attendance. In these instances it is the professional test maker, the teacher or trainer who determines the nature of the assessment – what form it takes, the content it will cover, when it will be administered, how it will be scored or graded.

Most of these assessments are also directly related to the subject matter being *taught*. The teacher or trainer 'teaches' certain materials and assumes that the students or trainees learn them. The assessment, therefore, serves as a check that the students have acquired the skills and knowledge facilitated by the teacher. In these traditional situations, the teacher or trainer maintains almost complete control over the assessment and the nature of the evidence used to draw the necessary inferences during the assessment process.

During APL assessments, however, the assessor *shares* control of the assessment process with the candidate. Although it is the assessor who makes the final decision regarding the outcome of the assessment, the candidate has considerable leeway in developing and presenting the evidence to be used in the assessment. Since APL assessments are not linked to any *particular* training or learning programme, it is assumed that a variety of evidence can be used during the assessment process. APL assessors, then, must come to anticipate and value the diversity of evidence that can be used by candidates to meet the standards or learning outcomes. Although assessors do not and cannot control the exact nature of the evidence candidates submit, they still must ensure that the evidence meets the technical requirements of any sound assessment.

Technical requirements

There are essentially five technical requirements that all APL assessments must meet. These include:

- validity
- reliability
- sufficiency
- authenticity
- currency.

Validity

Validity refers to how well the assessment matches what is being assessed. Consider, for example, the UK driving test. During the assessment the candidate is asked to drive the car under natural road conditions. While the candidate drives, the assessor notes how the individual handles the car, responds to road conditions and/or any emergencies that might crop up, performs particular manoeuvres and in general meets the specified standards of safe driving. A written test would not be considered a valid test of an individual's ability to drive a car.

Extending the example a bit further, however, some people argue that the driving test is not as valid as it should be since it does not test the driver's ability to drive on the motorways or at night. In this instance the examiner (assessor) gathers no direct information about the candidate's ability to drive in these situations. At the end of the road test, however, the examiner asks the driver a set of questions, some of which pertain to driving at night and on the motorway. These oral questions serve to test the candidate's knowledge and understanding from which the assessor draws further inferences about the candidate's ability. A candidate suffering from night blindness, though, might be able to answer the questions correctly but still be unable to drive safely in darkness. The oral examination then, while not in and of itself a valid assessment of a person's ability to drive, serves to extend the valid evidence collected during the actual road test, allowing the examiner to draw further inferences. For a number of reasons, not the least of which is cost, the day-time driving test is seen as sufficiently valid to allow a person who passes to drive under all circumstances.*

Another way of thinking about validity is to consider the notion of relevance. Is the evidence relevant or indicative of what is being assessed? Does the evidence match what is being looked for? Making sure the evidence is relevant – valid – is one way of contributing to 'getting the assessment right'. In many assessments – whether about people or things – there is an attempt to minimise the margin of error in the inferences being drawn. Using valid evidence is one of the most critical paths towards this desired goal.

Reliability

Reliability refers to the consistency of the assessment outcome. An assessment is considered reliable to the extent that different assessors using the same evidence make comparable judgements; or that the same assessor over time makes similar judgements. In APL, different candidates present different evidence. Thus in the context of APL, reliability is about assessors placing similar value on pieces of evidence and making similar judgements when confronted with the same evidence. Consider the following example: in a recent APL study, one of the awarding bodies identified a number of portfolios that had been assessed at Centre A towards a particular qualification. They then asked a group of equally trained assessors at Centre B to assess the same portfolios without knowledge of the decisions made by the assessors at Centre A. Once the portfolios were assessed by the second group, and the outcomes recorded, the awarding body research staff compared the results of the two assessments. They were pleased to find a high level of agreement among the

---

* Prior to taking the UK driving test, of course, the driving candidate must complete a statement regarding his or her health, including any problems with vision. Some problems, such as night blindness, would lead to restrictions being placed on the driver.

assessors regarding the decisions made about each portfolio, suggesting that the assessments were reliable.

In most norm-referenced assessment measures, reliabilities are presented as numerical indices linked to standard errors of measurement. In APL, there can be no numerical indices since each assessment is based on the unique evidence presented by individual candidates who work to predefined standards or learning outcomes. Non-numeric consistency of judgement is, perhaps, a more appropriate way of thinking about reliability in the APL context.

Sufficiency

As the word suggests, sufficiency relates to the *amount* of evidence needed during the assessment. It is impossible to give specific guidelines for sufficiency because in APL the evidence submitted by each candidate varies considerably. However, prior to beginning their assessments, APL assessors should try to establish rough guidelines for themselves (and the advisors and candidates), anticipating not only the types of evidence candidates might bring forward but the nature and amount that would be most acceptable in light of the requirements of the standards or the learning outcomes. Returning to the UK driving test, the practical part of the test is deemed not quite sufficient. And the oral questioning would fall far short of being sufficient. Trebling the time of the actual driving test to include motorway and night driving might provide sufficient evidence but at too high a cost. Extending the oral questioning would never make it sufficient (or valid). The current combination of the driving test *and* the oral questioning is assumed to provide sufficient evidence by which an assessor can judge whether or not an individual is competent to drive.

In constructing their portfolios, many adults tend to gather large amounts of the same type of evidence. They often believe that more is better. APL providers who do not offer adequate guidelines to candidates on the nature of acceptable evidence should not be surprised to receive vast amounts of overlapping or irrelevant evidence.

APL advisors need to help candidates select or generate the 'right' amount of evidence that will allow the assessors to complete the assessments. But it is the assessors who need to provide this information to the advisors either orally or, preferably, in writing. The advisors can then transmit the information to the candidates, either in the portfolio development workshops or in their one-to-one meetings. It is important to add that this information about assessment evidence will invariably change as assessors learn from experience about the evidence candidates can and do include in their portfolios.

Authenticity

Authenticity was highlighted in the last chapter. Essentially it refers to the 'ownership' of the evidence. Can the assessor be sure that the evidence presented in the portfolio really does represent the achievements of the candidate submitting it? In APL the issue of authenticity is of special concern because often the assessor may meet the candidate only at the time of assessment or perhaps not at all! It is essential that assessors verify not only the evidence produced by the candidate but sometimes the indirect evidence as well.

Most often a particular portfolio will contain a range of evidence. This combination of evidence frequently serves to verify the authenticity of any particular piece of evidence. As will be discussed later, there are a number of other ways that assessors can also confirm the authenticity of the evidence.

Currency

The concept of currency refers to the recency of the evidence. Assessors must be sure that the evidence submitted by candidates is current enough to be considered appropriate to the assessment. There are a number of interesting issues that need to be addressed concerning currency. The currency questions APL candidates most frequently ask are:

- how recent is recent?
- may I use evidence from three, five, ten years ago?

Again, the answers to these questions must be determined by the assessors. It is they who must use the standards or learning outcomes to provide the best guidance they can to candidates and advisors. In competency-based systems candidates generally receive recognition or credit for what they know and can do *now*. The evidence, therefore, must relate to their current performance. High technology fields in which rapid change is expected may require candidates to present evidence that is no more than one or two years old. Other disciplines may easily allow older evidence. Older evidence, even in high technology fields, may provide valuable information to the assessor about a particular candidate's background and learning progression. It can serve to strengthen a candidate's more recent evidence and can provide a more complete picture of what a candidate really knows and can do.

In their review of portfolios and in offering guidance to candidates and advisors, it is essential that assessors consider these five principles of assessment. Carefully adhered to, assessors can be assured of both the rigour and the credibility of their assessment decisions.

Applying the principles to the review of the portfolio

By the time the assessor receives the portfolio, the candidate will have had it reviewed for completeness by his or her advisor. Although it is not the advisor's job to assess the candidate, the advisor should be able to provide sufficient guidance to the candidates to ensure that their portfolios are well organised and readable; that the evidence is properly cross-referenced and presented in a logical fashion; and that the candidate has provided relevant information pertaining to authenticity and currency.

The assessor's task then is to begin the assessment process. This is usually accomplished in a number of steps:

1. *Familiarisation with the portfolio.* Assessors often find they need to begin the process by skimming the portfolio to get an idea of what it contains. They will want to read the personal report or narrative statement and any other overall introduction to the portfolio or the evidence that the candidate has provided. To no small degree, this first review of the portfolio is a bit like meeting a person for the first time: the assessor needs to get a general, overall impression.

2. *Making sure the expertise of the assessor is appropriate to the standards of learning outcomes.* Throughout this book, we have emphasised that all assessments must be led by the standards or learning outcomes. The assessors therefore need to make sure they are familiar with the standards or learning outcomes and that they have a clear notion of what they expect by way of evidence. If there is any question regarding this, they need to contact the advisor as soon as possible so that a more suitable assessor can be found.

3. *Reviewing the evidence.* Using the cross-referencing form(s), the assessor reviews the actual evidence, making sure that it is relevant to the standards or learning outcomes (validity); that it represents sufficient breadth and quality to be appropriate to the standards to which it applies (sufficiency); that it is, beyond a reasonable doubt, the work of the candidate (authenticity); and that it is recent enough to meet the requirements of the performance criteria or learning outcomes (currency).

To undertake this review, many assessors find it useful to develop and ask a series of key questions for each piece of evidence:

- *Validity*
  Does the evidence relate to the standards or learning outcomes the candidate is claiming?
  Does it match in part or all of the standards within a particular unit?
- *Sufficiency*

Can the evidence serve as conclusive proof for one or more of the units being assessed?

If not, what else would be required?

- *Currency*

Is the evidence sufficiently recent in light of the expectations of the standards?

- *Authenticity*

Is the direct evidence definitely the work of the candidate? Does the indirect evidence provide a true and accurate picture to support the candidate's learning claim?

The answers to each of these, or similar, questions will help the assessor to judge each piece of evidence against the criteria specified by the standards. Of course for each 'no', the assessor will need to ask at least two other questions:

- What else do I need to know before I am satisfied that the candidate is competent or has achieved the claimed learning outcomes?
- What is the best way of obtaining the evidence required?

For example, it may be that the evidence presented by the candidate is somewhat relevant to the standards or learning outcomes but does not fully reflect what is being sought. Or it may be that the evidence is highly relevant but several years old. Or perhaps the nature of the indirect evidence is not strong enough to fully support some of the other evidence in the portfolio. Or maybe the candidate has little or no evidence because of the highly confidential nature of the candidate's work.

Each of these situations, and dozens more, will require the assessor to develop a plan of action. This is called an initial assessment plan. If, on the other hand, the assessor believes that all of the criteria have been met and no further evidence is needed, the assessor can then recommend that the candidate receive the recognition or credit he or she is seeking.

The initial assessment plan

As assessors complete their reviews, they need to record their judgements and decisions. In so doing they create the assessment plan by which they will help the candidates collect or generate the necessary additional evidence that will enable the assessment to be completed. Several assessment options are available. These include: other artifacts or products; examples of indirect evidence; oral questioning; assignments or projects; demonstration; workplace assessment; or written tests. Figure 5.1, Assessor's Review Form, shows the way one APL centre required the assessors to record the outcomes of their review of the portfolio and develop their initial assessment plans which are then communicated and agreed with the candidates.

Additional artifacts or indirect evidence

Assessors frequently find that candidates can easily gather or produce additional artifacts that will satisfy the requirements of the assessment. This is one of the more expedient methods by which the assessment can be completed. Similarly, candidates may be able to request additional letters of validation or arrange for the assessor to speak with one or more of the people who have written on behalf of the candidate. In either case, the assessor needs to specify his or her request, give the candidate adequate time to produce the requested material and upon receipt of it continue with or complete the assessment.

In this context, letters of validation require highlighting. These letters can be essential to a candidate's learning claim. They can serve to describe the context, provide details, or evaluate the candidate's strengths and weaknesses. Although it is the candidate's responsibility to request and obtain these letters, it is important for assessors to continually review the letters they receive and redefine what makes some letters stronger than others. Candidates generally want to provide the strongest letters they can, but it is only with the guidance provided by the assessors and transmitted through the advisors that they will be able to do so.

The more confidence assessors have in the letters they receive,

Unit title <u>Information Processing</u>   Candidate name <u>Claire Thompson</u>

Element of Competence 1:

Create a database file on commercially-available software for recording, updating, manipulating and retrieving information.

Performance criteria

1

2

3

4

5

6

ASSESSOR'S REVIEW

Evidence assessed	Comments	Supplementary assessment recommended	Assessment completed
Evidence applicable to all performance criteria:			
Examples of work	Need to confirm currency	Oral questioning and/or demonstration	
Two letters of validation			
			Recommendation:
			Assessor's signature:
			Date:

Figure 5.1 *Assessor's Review Form*

Source: OU (1990) Unit 2, Module 2, p. 17.

the easier it will be to complete the candidate's assessment. After obtaining permission, therefore, the assessor should not hesitate to telephone the writer of a letter of validation to obtain additional information or to clarify particular issues.

Oral questioning
Oral questioning has several purposes in APL. It can be used to:

- clarify information;
- confirm process skills only suggested by the evidence;
- authenticate evidence;
- confirm current competence; and
- test for knowledge and understanding that cannot be inferred from the evidence already submitted.

Oral questioning is used extensively in almost all APL programmes. If the assessor believes that oral questioning would provide the required evidence, the candidate needs to be so notified and invited to meet (or speak on the telephone) with the assessor. If, as a result of oral questioning, the assessor still requires additional evidence, then other assessments as are described below will need to be negotiated and arranged.

Assignments or projects
Often candidates are unable to identify evidence from their past or current work environments or voluntary activities but they can complete specially designed assignments or projects. Like all evidence, the outcomes of the assignment or project must reflect the standards. Candidates required to complete assignments or projects must be provided with the necessary specifications – length, size, time or other parameters must all be spelled out. This form of assessment often plays a critical role for candidates with limited or no opportunities to gather or develop evidence from other sources.

Demonstration (including simulations and role play)
This form of assessment requires a special assessment occasion in which the assessor can observe the candidate performing a

particular set of activities or skills. Assessors using one or more of these methods will need to make sure that the candidate is aware of both the standards or learning outcomes against which he or she is to be assessed and the circumstances under which the assessment is to be conducted (time, place, other participants, etc). The validity of these methods depends on how well the assessor designs them.

Unlike most of the other options open to assessors, demonstrations, simulations and role plays often require significant planning and the use of extensive resources. Care must be taken by assessors to balance the cost of conducting an assessment by demonstration with the validity of the evidence generated.

Workplace assessment
In most situations workplace assessments generate extremely valid evidence, particularly when the assessment takes place in the normal course of events and is conducted by an internal assessor.

Workplace assessments are particularly useful in competency-based systems or in APL programmes in which the best evidence is being generated by the candidate in his or her own place of work. As Docking (1990a) reports, workplace assessments can significantly reduce some of the problems created by other forms of assessment. For example, it is not necessary to 'simulate' or create an artificial environment in which to assess the candidate; there is no need to create a special reassessment opportunity if the first assessment does not go as planned; there also is an opportunity to observe the candidate integrating many different aspects of his or her performance which may not be easy to infer from other forms of assessment.

However, if the assessor is external to the workplace, a number of other issues arise:

- the candidate may be nervous and not perform as well;
- there may be organisational, health, safety or legal restrictions that will limit the assessor's accessibility to the

candidate and detract from the validity of the assessment; and

- from the assessor's point of view, the time away from his or her normal workplace could create serious problems, not the least of which is cost.

Before agreeing to undertake assessments in the workplace, external assessors and their organisations will want to consider all of these factors. It may well be that if evidence is to be obtained from the workplace, the candidate will need to negotiate with his or her line manager to undertake an assessment and prepare a detailed letter of validation for the external APL assessor, who could then follow-up with minimal oral questioning, for example.

Written tests
Written tests may be useful when theories, knowledge or understanding cannot be inferred from other evidence. Although written tests are used extensively in traditional classrooms, APL assessors need to consider carefully issues of validity with such tests. Unless the assessor is assessing the candidate's writing performance, written examinations may not be appropriate – relevant – to the standards or learning outcomes.

In addition, it is important for assessors to remember that many adults will have been away from formal education and training for a long time. Since most will have been tested through written assessments, it is likely that many candidates will have a strong antipathy towards them and would prefer to be assessed by some other means if at all possible.

Recently some educational institutions have begun to think creatively about alternative evidence that could be used in place of conventional written assessments. Some examples are shown in Figure 5.2.

Obviously these various types of written work would need to relate to the standards, but just these few examples serve to illustrate the range of written evidence APL candidates can

Conventional assessment task	Alternative
Essay	Letter of advice to a Minister, a community action group or an employer. Magazine article prepared by the candidate. Book review prepared by the candidate.
Technical report	Tender for a contract.
Project report	Analysis of work problem with a written report.

Figure 5.2 *Alternative evidence*

include in their portfolios which may lessen the need for the assessor to require additional written assessment.

Assessment options

Clearly the number of different assessment techniques an assessor chooses to use will depend on a variety of factors. Most candidates' portfolios will contain a range of direct and indirect evidence and most assessors will use oral questioning for one purpose or another to supplement the main evidence provided in the portfolio. Ideally, it is most important for assessors to use the assessment techniques most appropriate to the needs of the individual candidates. For any given candidate, however, assessors should keep in mind that the range and quality of the evidence will vary considerably. Some candidates will be able to develop very strong portfolios that require no additional evidence or further assessment. At the other end of the spectrum will be candidates who have no products or even indirect evidence. These candidates will need to be assessed through one or more of the current assessment methods described above. And most candidates will fall somewhere in between, that is, they will have *some* evidence but will need to provide additional evidence or undergo further assessment to satisfy the expectations of the standards, and the assessor.

Organizational factors can also influence the choice of assessment options. These include the availability of resources, particular health and safety factors, and in some cases the organisational culture in which the APL programme is being offered. The cost of the assessment is another factor that assessors will want to weigh carefully as they work with APL candidates. Assessment costs can include not just the assessor's *and* the candidate's time, but also materials, accommodation, the time of other staff (eg, technicians or support staff), administrative processing, etc. Setting up a role play assessment for one candidate, for example, could be very expensive; if a number of candidates could be involved at the same time, then the cost might become more viable. Figure 5.3 illustrates the assessment process and assessment options just described.

Pitfalls in assessment

Contrary to existing myths, assessment is not an exact science. Even so-called objective tests are still dependent on human judgement for both their development and scoring. Given that all assessment relies heavily on the decisions and judgements of assessors, it may be helpful to the potential APL assessor to be conscious of some of the more common assessment pitfalls (Stewart, 1990). By being more aware of them, assessors can strive to avoid them! There are several worth highlighting:

The halo effect. This is a common type of error in which the assessors makes the assumption that if one piece of evidence is good or bad, all the candidate's evidence will be equally good or bad.

First impressions. In this situation, the assessor uses the assess-

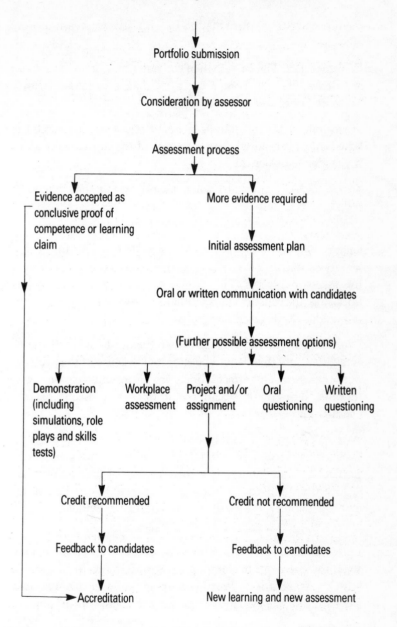

Figure 5.3 *Flowchart of the assessment process*

ment process to confirm that his or her initial impressions were correct.

Contrast effect. This arises when the outcomes of an assessment are determined by comparing a particular candidate with a preceding one, whether good or bad.

Stereotyping. This refers to judgements made about a candidate based on presupposed characteristics of the individual and/or the evidence presented.

Similar to me. This occurs when a candidate or the evidence is judged favourably because the assessor perceives a strong similarity between the candidate and him or herself.

Giving more weight to positives than to negatives. This may occur when a candidate's evidence or performance is contrary to what the assessor expects. This sometimes results in the assessor imposing unrealistic expectations on the candidate for the remainder of the assessment.

Experimenter effect. This occurs when the candidate performs or acts differently than would be expected because of the presence of the assessor. This effect is bound to be present to some degree in most assessment situations; it does not mean that the candidate's performance will be unacceptable.

Assessing progress rather than achievement. This occurs when the assessor pays too much attention to the effort or progress of a particular candidate, rather than to his or her attainments against the standards or learning outcomes. To the best of the assessor's ability, the candidate, and his or her evidence, should always be judged against the standards.

Lack of direction. In this instance assessors are not clear what it is they are assessing. It is important for assessors to be familiar with the standards or learning outcomes and know *in advance* the nature of the evidence or performance they are seeking.

Assessors answering their own questions. This occurs most often during oral assessments, particularly when assessors are not used to administering oral questions, are not familiar with the standards, or are uncomfortable in working with adults.

Illusion of validity. This occurs when the assessor feels good about his or her decision and therefore assumes it must be correct. However, this may mean that the assessor has found the evidence particularly interesting or the candidate particularly likeable rather than able.

Discriminatory practices. In assessment, as in other situations, this occurs when the assessor makes undue or unfair allowances or judgements for candidates because of race, gender, creed, sexual preference or special needs. Great care must be taken by APL assessors to make sure all candidates receive fair and equal opportunities during their assessments.

The assessor's role and responsibilities

In earlier chapters we reviewed and discussed the functions, roles and responsibilities of the advisors. It is important now to describe the roles and responsibilities of assessors. Thus far we have identified that the assessor has the prime responsibility for assessing APL candidates, determining whether or not they have met the standards or learning outcomes. But this is just one of the assessor's responsibilities. Attention must be paid to the other aspects of the assessor's work.

Developing and using standards

Throughout this book continued reference has been made to standards or learning outcomes. They are the kingpin to sound APL assessments. Many professionals working in Britain are beginning to use the new National Vocational Qualifications (NVQ) framework which provides standards of occupational competence for a wide range of occupations. These standards are becoming part of normal training and educational provision

117

and are serving as a basis for significant changes in the curriculum and in assessment methodology.

In the context of this book, the standards provide ready opportunities for adults who wish to earn one or more NVQs (or SVQs in Scotland). Candidates, their advisors and the assessors all have access to standards. There are no hidden expectations lurking behind the minds of particular teachers or trainers. The standards are explicit, assessable, related to occupational competence and available for all to use. APL assessments in the NVQ framework, therefore, have a clear focus: candidates are expected to prove their occupational competence as described by the units and elements of competence with their associate performance criteria.

Assessors working outside the context of NVQs, however, may find that there are no explicit standards or learning outcomes by which they can assess candidates. Although they may be recognising candidates' prior learning for purposes of access, exemption or placement, often their decisions are based more on 'gut feelings' or time-serving rather than explicit standards.

Professionals seriously wanting or needing to offer a sound APL service need to begin by developing standards or learning outcomes (Simosko, 1988). This must be perceived as one of the primary responsibilities of assessors. Since they are the subject specialists, only they can develop the content specifications or standards. Through one method or another they need to decide what is important about their discipline or occupation and from that spell out their expectations in the form of observable and assessable criteria. As summarised by Mitchell and Johnson (1987), 'Assessment is about generating evidence and making judgments (about) an individual's competence, by comparing his or her performance against established criteria'. APL assessors working in environments or contexts that lack clear standards must lay the groundwork for their assessments by developing them.

Whether assessors are concerned with academic disciplines or occupational standards it is always possible to define the standards or expectations of the successful candidate. Often traditional educators argue that setting standards is acceptable for vocational areas but not for more theory-based fields; or they argue that a particular discipline is too complex to describe in terms of standards or learning outcomes. Yet every discipline and occupation *can* be analysed to develop clear, assessable standards. Knowledge, skills and understanding can all be articulated and assessed, at least to some degree. It may take time and patience to complete the analysis and develop the standards or learning outcomes, but it is possible. Professionals implementing APL will need to explore one or more of the available methods by which to complete this work.

Providing feedback to candidates

Another primary responsibility of the assessor is to provide feedback to candidates. This comes in at least two places in the APL assessment process: after the initial review of the portfolio and at the end of each completed assessment. Candidates need to be told what has been accepted and what more, if anything, is needed. They also need directions regarding any further assessments: they need to have a clear idea of what will be looked for during the assessment and what the particular situation will entail. Lastly, of course, they need to be advised of the outcome of the overall assessment.

Assessors should provide feedback as clearly and constructively as possible. Even if the evidence in a portfolio is not sufficient or does not meet other technical requirements, the assessor should acknowledge that for most candidates the production of the portfolio represents a considerable amount of time, effort and emotional investment. Assessors should try to convey their respect for the effort of the candidate even when the evidence is lacking in one or more ways.

Similarly at the end of any particular current assessment or at the end of the overall assessment period, if the candidate has not proved that he or she has met the standards or learning outcomes, the assessor must convey the news, but in a way that will encourage the candidate rather than undermine his or her continued efforts. In 'putting the customer first', assessors may need to remind themselves that the primary purpose of APL is to promote the development of the individual – to help him or her reach an important goal. Because a candidate was not successful in his or her attempt to receive the sought recognition or credit does not mean that the candidate should be deflected from continuing to work toward the desired goal. The way in which assessors provide feedback will be critical to how candidates feel about the overall process and often themselves. Assessors should therefore carefully consider the way in which they provide feedback to candidates. In this context it is especially important that assessors demonstrate a lack of bias or discrimination.

Maintaining records

Another responsibility of assessors is to prepare and maintain records for each assessment they complete. This will involve recording the outcomes of the review of the portfolio and any subsequent assessment. It may also require the assessor to tape-record and store the outcomes of any oral assessments. Since assessors are very much a part of the overall quality assurance process, their records must be clear, accurate and complete for every candidate they assess.

Communicating with other professionals

Another essential responsibility of the assessor is to communicate effectively on a regular basis with a range of other professionals. These include the advisors, other assessors, internal or external verifiers, and administrative or management staff.

Advisors
Since it is the advisors who support candidates throughout the APL process, it is essential that they are as well informed as possible. Assessors must therefore make sure that they meet and

talk with the advisors on an on-going basis to keep them well briefed and to provide an opportunity to discuss particular issues or concerns. The better prepared the advisors are, the more likely it is that assessors will receive well organised and stronger portfolios and candidates who understand the nature of evidence and the expectations of any further assessments.

Assessors need to remember that in most contexts advisors are not technical experts. They cannot and do not make technical or academic judgements. However, with support from the assessors, they can go a long way in helping candidates interpret the standards, select or generate evidence and meet the overall requirements of the assessment.

The advisors may also wish the assessor to participate in either an APL briefing session or a portfolio development workshop. In these instances the advisor and the assessor will need to agree the exact role and contribution expected of the assessor.

Other assessors

Communication with other assessors either from within the same centre or across centres is also essential to a strong and credible APL programme. Assessors need to learn from one another: they need to know that they are interpreting the standards in a similar fashion, that they agree on the nature of acceptable evidence, and that they are meeting the needs of individual candidates in similarly effective and sensitive ways.

It is also useful for assessors to meet assessors from different disciplines or occupational areas. Often the cross-fertilisation that occurs provides new information, perspectives and problem-solving techniques. Many assessors, particularly from academic organisations, find that meeting with subject specialists from other disciplines stimulates their thinking and encourages them to be more creative in addressing a range of assessment issues.

Internal or external verifiers

In some situations, such as further education in Britain, assessors need to provide information and feedback to both internal and external verifiers as part of the quality assurance process. The primary purpose of the verifiers is to ensure that the standards have been met; that the assessments have been conducted in a fair and reliable way; and that any outstanding issues regarding the specifications or interpretation of the standards are identified.

Administrators and managers

Very often assessors are called upon to meet administrators or managers who want to know how the APL process is going. They may want to collect data on candidates, evidence, units assessed and any number of other things and discuss these matters with the assessors. Keeping clear and accurate records, working closely with advisors, other assessors and verifiers, will help each assessor on the APL team meet the administrative and management needs of his or her organisation.

The role and responsibilities of assessors may vary in degree from one organisation to another. However, in all contexts assessors will be expected to meet a range of technical and communication requirements and should be prepared to respond to the needs of individual candidates, colleagues, and their own organisations.

Summary

Sound assessments are critical to the development of an APL service. APL assessors must adhere to a range of principles of good practice. These include making sure the evidence submitted and/or generated by candidates is valid, reliable, sufficient, authentic and recent enough to be of value to the assessment.

As part of their review of portfolios, assessors will need to convey to candidates either orally or in writing the outcomes of the assessment and develop initial assessment plans for each candidate as necessary. Following the review of evidence in the portfolio, assessors may need to ask candidates to generate additional evidence through oral questioning, demonstrations or other techniques. In conducting these assessments, assessors must be wary of a range of assessment pitfalls.

The assessor's role and responsibilities extend beyond assessing candidates. In some cases assessors may need to develop standards or learning outcomes and always they will be expected to give constructive feedback to candidates, maintain records, and communicate with other professionals about their work.

Chapter 6

Implementing APL

Thus far we have looked at the purpose and benefits of APL and the key roles and responsibilities of advisors and assessors. In this chapter we will investigate implementation issues, those concrete, practical issues that must be addressed before a sound APL service can be introduced. Many organisations find that APL can be integrated easily into their normal provision; others find that APL itself acts as a catalyst for much needed change.

The suggestions offered here are not intended to be prescriptive – because every organisation has its own distinct needs and ways of doing things – but, as Rosabeth Moss Kanter (1985) suggests, there is a lot organisations can learn from the innovation and success of others. This chapter is based largely on the experiences of dozens of organisations in both North America and Britain that have developed strong, exciting APL programmes that have served not only the needs of the adults making use of the service but the needs and interests of the organisation as well.

Organisational purpose

A college, university, employer or other training provider wishing to introduce APL should carefully consider its reason for wanting to do so. Does it want to:

- attract new students, employees or trainees?
- motivate existing client groups?
- add APL to a range of other learner- or customer-oriented services?
- use APL to create a range of new services and a new image?
- maximise the effective use of learning or training provision already on offer?
- develop new partnerships with other organisations?

All of these are examples of why some organisations have chosen to develop and introduce an APL service. They have identified an organisational need that they felt could be met by APL. But it is one thing to *want* to do something and quite another to actually do it. For many organisations the bridge between the two is often an over-arching review or organisational audit. This self-assessment allows the organisation to analyse its mission, policies and procedures and from that, develop an institutional action plan which will facilitate the introduction of APL with its incumbent services and structures.

APL and the organisational audit

As we have seen throughout this book, the concept of APL is based on several assumptions which frequently do not characterise traditional education and training programmes. APL requires a different emphasis within the organisation and the roles and functions of staff can differ significantly. Some examples of these differences are shown in Figure 6.1.

Once organisations realise that some of the requirements of APL differ from those of their normal delivery system, they begin to see the need for the institutional audit.

A sound audit will investigate how well the organisation is placed for delivering APL. This will include a thorough analysis of:

- the overall mission of the organisation;

Traditional	APL
• Organisation provides *learning* and assessment opportunities.	• Organisation provides *assessment* and learning opportunities.
• Policies and procedures often based on historical justifications and administrative convenience.	• Policies and procedures based on needs of learners within constraints of the organisation.
• Assessment is linked to particular learning or training programme.	• Assessment is not linked to any particular learning or training programme.
• Subject specialist is first and foremost a teacher.	• Subject specialist is first and foremost an assessor.
• No necessary separation of advising, teaching and assessing roles.	• Separation of advising, teaching and assessing roles required.

Figure 6.1 *Differences between traditional and APL educational and training programmes*

- the premises and accommodation;
- the written and visual information provided by the centre;
- the skills and training needs of the staff;
- the organisation and availability of the training, learning and assessment offerings;
- the nature of the learners making use of the services of the centre;
- the framework by which learners progress through the system;
- costs and fees; and
- the management structure.

By looking at each of these and learning from the experience of others, professionals wanting to implement APL will have some guidance as to how to proceed.

What follows is a brief analysis of each of these areas, highlighting key factors that potential APL providers will need to consider. A list of questions has also been offered to help the reader design and conduct his or her own organisational audit. Although the type and range of questions a centre might ask itself will vary, those presented suggest useful areas for exploration. From the outcomes of the audit, a centre can develop its own implementation or action plan for introducing – or improving – its APL service.

Mission

Almost all organisations have a mission. Some even have a mission statement. The great pity is, however, that often the mission and the mission statement do not support one another. And of course, many organisations do not have any mission statement or even a clear statement of purpose.

As part of its audit, one college in North America discovered that its mission statement had not been reviewed or changed in ten years. The original statement reflected the college's purpose which was basically to attract and educate traditional-aged students right out of high school for the primary purpose of equipping them to become 'better citizens'. In the course of the ten years, however, many changes had taken place within the college, largely as a result of significant demographic changes in the area. The college now enrolled as many people over the age of 25 as it did those under 25 and a large percentage of its resources was spent on meeting the basic skills needs of a significant population of new immigrants. It also offered a wide variety of vocational programmes, unknown ten years ago.

In this particular case, the lack of an appropriate mission statement did not undermine the college's ability to respond effectively to changing circumstances. But not all organisations are so lucky. The lack of an appropriate mission statement may not only limit the organisation's ability to attract the customers it wants, it may also contribute to on-going debate among staff as to what they should be doing in their jobs.

The changing role of further education in the UK provides an apt example of this. Ten years ago further education colleges served basically two purposes: (1) to support apprenticeship training programmes and (2) to deliver full-time courses for those school leavers unable to get into higher education. The current-day structures and policies of many colleges are still geared to meeting these purposes. Yet regularly colleges are finding that they must meet the needs of increasingly diverse populations, including more adult returners; that people want greater flexibility in both learning and assessment opportunities; that local employers expect the college to deliver a range of short courses; NVQs must be offered alongside more traditional qualifications; and all the while colleges are being expected to operate increasingly on a full-cost recovery basis. It is no wonder that staff – managers, lecturers, and support staff – often feel overwhelmed and confused.

The more innovative colleges are taking a hard look at what they *can* and *want* to deliver and are identifying their primary client groups. From that they are developing sound mission statements to describe their purposes, roles and ultimate objectives. These statements – hopefully developed and agreed by large numbers of the staff – serve as the primary vehicles by which the college lets its various customers (potential clients, employers, awarding bodies and others) learn about its objectives and commitments.

In the context of APL, which is a highly learner-centered service, the organisation's mission statement ideally should embrace the notion of facilitating the development of each individual it serves; of providing flexible learning and assessment opportunities; and of delivering a range of integrated, complimentary programmes designed to meet the needs of particular client groups.

Selected Questions

1. Does the centre have a mission statement?
2. If so, does it reflect an orientation to include adults?
3. Does it highlight the centre's flexibility of programmes and services for individual learners?
4. Does it clearly indicate that programmes and services for all learners, including adults, are integrated?
5. Is the language meaningful and jargon free?

Premises and accommodation

Part of the audit must also look at the nature of the physical plant in which the APL service is to be located. Many centres take their premises for granted and do not realise how inhospitable they often have become. Vast resources are often spent on keeping places looking cold and uninviting. One college principal was astounded at the initial reluctance of staff to the suggestion that students' art work be displayed around the college, not just in the corridors near the art department. Staff long-accustomed to the barren off-white walls (which were regularly painted and maintained) argued that: 'students will deface the art work'; 'hanging the pictures will be expensive'; 'the stuff isn't that good'; 'this isn't a museum, it's a college!' But the principal's decision prevailed. The art and design students organised the display of the work as an extension or their ongoing classroom work; staff and students alike were amazed at the high level of creativity and diversity of the work; and after several months, staff and visitors alike looked forward to the changing 'show.'

This is but one small example of the way in which one APL centre began to make its environment more friendly and welcoming. By displaying the students' art work the college was publicly supporting its mission statement by saying that people count and that the organisation valued the diversity of its contributing members.

Why, you may be asking, is this so critical to the success of APL? The reason is simple: the environment offered by an

organisation is one of the most important outward manifesta-
tions of its mission statement. An organisation committed to
fostering the development of individuals needs to welcome
those individuals and make them feel that the place itself is there
to be *used* and *enjoyed*. It is not a prison; people, especially adults,
come there of their own volition. All too many centres
professing a commitment to learner-centredness do little to
demonstrate this commitment in their premises.

If we remember earlier discussions about APL candidates,
many of whom carry long-standing fears and hostilities about
education, training and assessment, it becomes the centre's
responsibility to make sure those people are treated in a way that
will facilitate their progression. One way to do that is to make
sure the environment is inviting and comfortable.

When asked what they liked most about the physical
environment of their APL centres, adults from several different
nations representing various levels and contexts of education
and training have said:

- There were clear directions to everything I needed.
- Parking was available.
- When I first went in I was pleased to see plants and
  pictures. It wasn't anything like I expected.
- It was bright and airy. I didn't feel closed in.
- The information I needed was right where my advisor said
  it would be.
- The receptionist smiled and seemed genuinely friendly.
- I chose my centre because it has child-minding facilities.
- Everyone's name is visible when you go into the office.

Except for the parking and child-minding facilities, none of
these observations required a large outlay of money by the
providing organisation, yet all contributed to making the adults
(and no doubt others) feel welcome. These comments, and
others like them, reflect a belief among candidates that they
selected the right place for the help and services they required.

Selected Questions

1. Are key offices well sign-posted outside and inside the building(s)?
2. Is there adequate parking and/or public transport when the centre is open?
3. Are the interiors of the buildings light, airy and well ventilated?
4. Is access available to all offices, toilets and other facilities for disabled people?
5. Have receptionists, security guards and others been trained to greet and respond to the questions of potential candidates?
6. Are facilities open and staffed in the evenings and at the weekends?

Written and visual material

The very term APL is an example of accepted international jargon. Although we have used it throughout this book, centres were urged earlier to develop other ways of describing the service. This suggestion is not just appropriate to APL. So much of the language colleges, universities and training centres use is riddled with language that is élitist, unnecessarily verbose, and unclear.

A centre wanting to introduce APL must conduct a review of all of its written and visual material. Again, the tone, clarity and visual presentation should each serve to reflect the mission of the organisation and the commitment of the people working within that institution.

Although many aspects of the audit can be well conducted by groups of staff members across the institution, the review of the written and visual materials often requires the involvement of outsiders as well. Those within a given organisation may see nothing 'wrong' or misleading about particular words, phrases, or visual images because they have been so close to it for a long period of time. It often takes the views of outsiders to highlight the inadequacies of publications.

This review does not always require the outside expertise of a professional editor or consultant. Many APL centres (and other truly learner-centred organisations) request on-going feedback from their various client groups to make sure the language of their publications is relevant to the needs and aspirations of particular client groups, understandable, and non-discriminatory. Properly designed questionnaires, completed by candidates (whether students, trainees or employees), can provide valuable information which will enable a centre to revise, modify or do away with some aspects of its publications or other visual materials.

Selected Questions

1. Do the visual images of publications reflect the diversity of the various client groups served by the organisation?
2. Are the words used jargon-free and easy to understand?
3. Is regular feedback from candidates collected, analysed and used to modify materials?
4. Is there an internal editorial committee or board which meets regularly to review and update the materials of the organisation?

Skills and training needs of staff

As we have seen, APL requires the services of trained advisors and assessors. It is therefore essential that a centre wishing to offer APL consider the strengths of its existing staff before embarking on any particular training programme. To no small degree, the centre needs to conduct an 'audit' of its staff. This doesn't mean just tallying up the number of degrees and other qualifications of the staff. It means taking a hard look at the particular skills and strengths of the staff and from that determining further training needs.

For example, almost all teachers and trainers, regardless of the level or context in which they work, do assessment. Yet very few have had any formal training as assessors. Teacher training programmes may include some input on assessment, but only rarely is assessment conceived of as something more than written tests designed to test candidates' or students' knowledge. Very few people have been trained to consider a diversity of evidence in their assessments; even fewer have been trained to use standards or learning outcomes as the basis of their assessments. Indeed experience suggests that there is a genuine lack of understanding about the basic principles of assessment and that much of the assessment candidates are subjected to is based on a strong set of myths (Docking, 1990b). For example, many traditional subject specialists who teach or train really believe the following:

Myth: That assessment must be a competitive process, pitting one learner against another, and that collaborative effort is tantamount to 'cheating'.

Myth: That the excellence of the few can only be attested by the failure of the many.

Myth: That assessment should be a retrospective, summative and terminating process.

Myth: That grades (A,B,C,D; deciles; percentiles, etc) can faithfully and meaningfully reflect performance in a unit of study or over a collection of units.

Myth: That assessment processes must be hidden and secret from the learner (and often the trainer) if fairness is to be ensured.

Myth: That knowledge alone can be an adequate indicator of real performance.

Myth: That assessment methods should be devised to heighten the fear of failure and the hope of success as motivating strategies for comprehensive and effective learning.

Myth: That anxiety and pain are necessary accompaniments to rigorous assessment.

All of these myths – so deeply believed by many professional educators and trainers – are contrary to the successful implementation of APL and a range of other learner-centred services. Compare the following characteristics of APL with the myths listed above:

APL: Assessment is not competitive; each candidate has an equal chance to demonstrate his or her competence or strengths.

APL: APL encourages excellence in *each* person coming forward. As a process it helps people identify their own strengths and weaknesses.

APL: APL assessments *are* retrospective and summative; they are not generally 'terminating'. For most APL candidates, the assessment represents some sort of a new beginning.

APL: APL assessments cannot be graded (although some colleges and universities artificially do assign grades). APL candidates working to clearly stated and assessable standards or learning outcomes either meet the standards or don't.

APL: In APL it is *essential* that learners know what is expected of them. The assessment criteria cannot be hidden or secret; otherwise the candidate is unable to match his or her strengths to the standards on offer or prepare for assessment.

APL: While separate knowledge assessments are often important in APL, they represent only a portion of most assessments.

APL: Assessment in APL is designed to *lessen* fear of failure by giving candidates control of the evidence and encouraging their self-confidence.

APL: The use of advisors and an openness about the assessment process have been found to reduce the anxiety and pain often associated with traditional assessment and helps adults overcome long-standing fears about their 'assessment inadequacies.'

This is just one example of the type of staff strength or weakness that needs to be identified during the audit. Obviously the staff's beliefs about assessment, adult learners generally, and flexible learning options all need to be profiled. If large numbers of staff do not think that APL will work, it won't!

Although this example has focused on the area of assessment, a similar example could be developed about advising or managing the APL service. Simply by way of example, many highly trained advisors think it is their job to tell candidates what to do: they tell them what courses to take, which lecturer they might find best, what qualification to seek. APL advisors, on the other hand, must be willing to give control to the learner and provide on-going support and guidance as necessary. Many advisors, long accustomed to working with young people, find it difficult at first to actually negotiate fully with the adults they meet through APL. Once they do, of course, they often report much higher job satisfaction since frequently the interactions with the APL candidates are so positive.

Similarly many managers believe that to manage properly they must distance themselves from those on their teams. The delivery of APL requires close team work between the advisors, assessors and managers. More effective managers regularly provide team-building opportunities for their staff.

The audit, then, needs to identify the technical strengths the staff could bring to the APL service. Because the process can represent such a radical departure from the way much traditional assessment works, it must also reveal staff willingness to try something new – be that working with adults or working as a team.

Selected Questions

1. Have subject specialists been trained to use a variety of evidence in their assessments?
2. Have all staff been trained to develop and/or use standards of competence or learning outcomes?
3. Do staff regularly work with adults or will they need orientation to the needs of adults?
4. Are advisors trained to lay out options and give candidates control of their own decisions?

5. Do staff participate in regular, on-going team-building exercises?
6. Is professional development about APL and related initiatives made available to staff and is it properly resourced?

Availability of advising, learning, and assessment offerings

APL requires significant flexibility in the delivery of services. An organisation wishing to implement APL, therefore, needs to determine whether it is adequately flexible to meet the needs of most candidates and potential groups of candidates. The audit needs to consider at least three areas: advising, learning and assessment services.

In Chapters 3 and 4 we looked at the range of services offered by advisors. But the audit needs to look at the structure in which the advisors function, the range of other responsibilities they have and the time allocated to deliver the service. All too often centres embark on APL without careful consideration of these issues and find they have created an organisational nightmare for the staff and the candidates.

For example, at one college in England, it was decided that the APL advisors should be linked to particular departments. Therefore a catering specialist would work with catering candidates; an engineering specialist with the engineers; music specialist with musicians, and so forth. What the college failed to anticipate was that:

1. candidates would come seeking recognition or credit in more than one area;
2. some candidates would arrive uncertain about whether they had any 'creditable' learning;
3. an unspoken competitiveness would develop among the departments about recruiting APL candidates;
4. subject specialists were not adequately prepared to provide sound and on-going support and guidance; and

5. without a central administrative office to monitor the progress of each candidate, there was no way the centre could evaluate the effectiveness of the advising services candidates were receiving.

Before piloting APL, centre staff had engaged in significant debate about whether or not non-specialist staff could serve as advisors. Lecturers did not think APL would work if they themselves were not in control so the decision was taken to give the departments control of the advising function. As might be expected, the centre was not successful in sustaining the programme and the few candidates who did receive credit did so largely though current assessments which were often the same classroom tests used by the advisor!

By contrast another college set up an APL advising service as part of its career services unit. The advisors were trained counsellors not linked to any particular department. They worked comfortably with a range of candidates who were interested in seeking recognition in many diverse fields and drew on the expertise of the assessors at the regularly scheduled team meetings and on a one-to-one basis as needed. Candidates at this centre had only one advisor, regardless of how many different areas they were seeking credit for; the advisors were able to work as easily with candidates who were uncertain about whether to go forward for APL as with those who were sure; no competitiveness developed between or among departments; the advisors were adequately prepared and accustomed to providing the types of support and help candidates needed; the advising office itself served as the administrative coordination function so the progress of each candidate could be carefully monitored; and lastly, there was a clear distinction between the role of the advisor and that of the assessor.

Centres considering the implementation of APL will want to look at their own structure and determine the best way to offer the advising services.

Thus far in this book we have said little about new learning. Yet for many APL candidates the acquisition of new skills and knowledge is critical to their overall development plans. They want to receive recognition or credit for what they already know and can do so that they can get on to something else. In Britain as in certain quarters in North America the issue of providing new learning has been one of the biggest impediments to the implementation of APL, primarily because the educational structure is not sufficiently flexible to allow learners to gain the 'bits and pieces' of new learning they may require to complete a unit or qualification.

Ideally all centres offering APL should have a unitised or modularised curriculum which will allow candidates to drop in and out as needed. They should also offer a range of open or distance learning options and should be able to offer flexible workshops which will help candidates 'top up' on an informal basis. But this is the ideal and in most contexts very far from the reality and constraints of education-based centres. Industrial training organisations and employers often do have modularised training with distance or open learning components but, as would be expected, these offerings are not always in the areas needed or wanted by the candidate.

The implementation of NVQs in England, Wales and Northern Ireland, and National Certificates and SVQs in Scotland, will make the situation a little easier for many colleges. No longer will they be restricted to offer one- or two-year courses, but rather will have smaller units around which to develop their curriculum. But even once in place, colleges will still need to decide how to help candidates achieve an entire unit, if candidates can, for example, only prove competence for four out of five elements of competence. This need not always be a problem: some learners, for example, are happy to take more responsibility and creatively develop themselves either in or out of the workplace.

Employers helping their employees earn NVQs and wishing to make use of APL also will have to address how to provide opportunities by which their employees can develop new skills in the workplace. Employers need to remember that assessment is but one part of the learning process. Learning opportunities must be agreed and facilitated that will allow candidates to progress in keeping with the needs of the organisation and based on what the employees already know and can do.

In North America the credit-hour system does provide for considerable modularisation when compared with the British system. But even there, the issue arises: since APL is basically offered only in colleges and universities and often, it must be said, without benefit of clear standards or learning outcomes, candidates frequently have heavy knowledge and understanding assessments to undergo. Although many adults are rich in experiences and indeed would far exceed the performance of recent graduates, they often lack the required text-book theory material that is so deeply entrenched in American higher education. One college in the Midwest received federal support to offer only the theory-based material of a range of traditional courses. APL candidates could come in the evenings for the segments they felt they needed during the time they were developing their portfolios. By the time they were ready to undergo assessment, most felt adequately prepared to take the knowledge-based assessments. As valuable as the programme was, however, regrettably the college was not able to sustain it once the initial funding was exhausted.

One model which seems to overcome many of the obstacles of further and higher education can be found in some of the more successful skills training centres in Britain. Many offer the same qualifications as traditional colleges but do so in a way that is both flexible and efficient. Trainees are assessed before they receive training so that both the trainee and the trainers know in advance what his or her other strengths are. Then, because the delivery is already modularised and delivered in on-going workshops, APL candidates can attend only those sessions they need to meet the requirements of the full qualification.

The area of providing new learning will be a challenge to most readers of this book. And indeed, professionals throughout the world are addressing many of these, and other, issues. Many APL providers are seeking new partnerships in an attempt to come up with positive solutions. As the total quality management example in Chapter 2 demonstrates, partnerships may be the most useful way forward in this area.

Centres deciding to offer APL should at least be clear on the available options they can offer candidates. Again, the audit will serve to highlight both the strengths of any given institution and also gaps or weaknesses.

Assessment too needs to be delivered in a flexible manner and at times convenient to both the candidates and the assessors. Experience has shown that the biggest hurdle here is one of time: assessors who generally have teaching or training responsibilities as well need to be allocated sufficient time and resources to undertake the assessments. This too is a matter that is sufficiently complex to cause some apprehension about the cost-effectiveness of APL.

What has become obvious in recent years is that to deliver an effective APL service, the roles of traditional educators and trainers need to be modified. Once the roles are more clearly described and agreed with the staff (and sometimes local government organisations, unions, and others), it becomes much easier to *reallocate* resources. The implementation of APL and other learner-centred services may not require more money but it will most assuredly require a different distribution.

Selected Questions

1. Is there a central office that provides the advising function to APL candidates?
2. Are staff and candidates clear about the way in which portfolios and candidate records are processed and maintained?
3. Are candidates able to make use of a wide variety of learning resources, including distance and open learning, flexible workshops, or individualised learning programmes?
4. Are partnerships in place whereby the centre can cost-effectively increase its new-learning options to candidates?
5. Are new-learning options available in the evenings and/ or at weekends?

6. Are professional staff given time to develop the materials they need to support adults wanting or needing new learning?

Nature of learners

This will probably be the easiest analysis to undertake as part of the audit. Most centres are well aware of the number and type of students or trainees they recruit. More difficult in the context of APL is the nature of the candidates a centre would like to attract. Often centres come to APL because they want to expand their services to adults, attract more of them, and meet the needs of local employers. Before a sound APL service can be implemented, centres need to think about the likely strengths and needs of particular groups. For example, as groups, experienced managers and semi-skilled unemployed people might make very different demands on the staff within an APL centre. One might be able to progress through the process with well-written guidelines and checklists whereas the other might require extensive one-to-one support. The audit should help centres clarify their current clients and identify any new groups that could be served by an APL service.

Selected Questions

1. Do recruitment efforts aim at groups of people as reflected in the mission statement?
2. Have centre materials been designed to attract adults?
3. Has the centre formed partnerships with other organisations in an effort to attract candidates who could most benefit from the APL service?
4. Are regular briefing sessions or workshops held in the community to provide potential candidates with information about APL and other learner-centred services?
5. Is there systematic follow-up of all people who contact the centre but do not enrol?

Framework by which learners progress through the system

Centres considering APL should remember that the basic purpose is to facilitate the progression of individuals. To that end, the centre needs to try to simplify its procedures and reduce red tape. This is often easier said than done! But the audit should reveal the points of tension between the needs of individuals and the needs of the administrative structure.

Clearly stated policies can go a long way to help candidates *and staff* understand the APL model once in place. An APL centre needs to have policies in place regarding:

- fees;
- top-up learning;
- time frame for portfolio development;
- nature (and in some contexts amount) of credit that can be awarded;
- appeals procedures; and
- type of records retained about each candidate.

These policies should be consistent with other policies developed by the centre and should not in any way marginalise either the staff who deliver the APL services or the candidates themselves. APL works best when it is integrated with other programmes and services a centre may offer. The audit should serve to reveal where APL easily 'fits' and where modifications are needed to existing policies.

Selected Questions

1. Is the fee structure clear, easy to understand and fair in light of other charges the centre makes?
2. Are policies clear and precise as to the nature and amount of credit candidates can earn?
3. Are new-learning options provided at times and in a manner needed by APL candidates?
4. Are time frames set and agreed with staff and candidates?
5. Is there a sound appeals process in place?

6. Are the records developed and maintained for each candidate clear and in keeping with all legislation regarding the confidentiality of data?

Costs and fees

Resourcing APL is another key factor in its implementation. Centres will need to review and analyse all relevant cost factors in order to develop a strategy for setting fees. Experience has shown that there are different cost features related to the start up of the service and the actual offering of the service.

For example, during the start-up phase the centre will need to consider staff development, the production of materials, the purchase of equipment, and accommodation. Some of these cost features, however, may already be paid for by one or more other programmes or services, eg, equipment and accommodation. So the audit will need to determine what *new* costs will be associated with the development of an APL service.

The costs associated with the delivery of the service will also need to be analysed. These include:

- the staffing of the service, eg advisor(s), assessor(s), manager or coordinator, and support staff;
- accommodation, eg, advising area(s), assessment area(s), storage area(s) and any newly-created open learning area;
- equipment;
- consumables, eg, telephone, postage, forms, tapes, other printed matter like brochures and guides for candidates;
- marketing or promotion materials, including items for briefing and portfolio development workshops; and
- external validation and/or verification.

Not included in this list is the provision of new-learning opportunities because it is assumed that these options will be drawn on by a range of learners, not just APL candidates.

There are a number of ways that an APL service can be financed (Kendall, 1990).

1. The service can be priced on a full-cost-recovery basis.
2. The service can serve as a loss leader to attract new learners to the centre.
3. The centre may want to charge a fee equivalent to the mainstream delivery of courses, modules or training programmes.
4. The centre may want to charge groups of users according to what the market will bear.
5. The centre may want to charge for each part of the service separately, eg, advising and per unit assessed (not accredited!), etc.

Figure 6.2 provides a description of the advantages and possible limitations of each of these strategies.

Selected Questions

1. Has the centre developed an APL model and identified the cost factors associated with each?
2. Has the centre compared possible costs and fees of APL with those of other services and programmes of the centre?
3. Is the pricing structure based on sound reasoning and consistent with candidates' ability to pay?

The management structure

Once again, the audit needs to dip into a sensitive area, that of the management structure! For APL to work effectively, it must be delivered through an effective team approach and the management of both the organisation and the APL service itself should reflect the values conveyed in the mission statement.

Increasingly colleges, universities, training organisations and employers are exploring the idea of Total Quality Management (TQM) as was briefly mentioned in Chapter 2. Interest in TQM seems to reflect a growing need within organisations to make staff more responsive not just to the requirements of the external customers or clients but to the needs of the staff as

Strategy	Advantages	Limitations
1. Full cost recovery	1. Service pays for itself 2. Clients do not undervalue the service 3. Development costs taken into account 4. Stimulates effective use of resources	1. Could be unfairly treated compared to subsidised courses 2. Some clients who would benefit may be lost 3. Often difficult to calculate overheads
2. Loss leader	1. Attracts more customers 2. Encourages use of other service 3. Brings wider benefits to the community	1. Service must be funded from elesewhere 2. Resources may become overstretched 3. People may not continue on to conventional courses or service 4. Service may be perceived as 'cheap' option
3. Equivalent to mainstream charge	1. Easy to administer – no separate arrangements required 2. Variances to clients (eg, unemployed, ET, corporate) already within system 3. May turn out to be cheaper to operate than mainstream	1. No financial saving possible to the client 2. No account of development costs taken 3. May turn out to be more expensive to operate than mainstream 4. Some candidates may feel over-charged
4. Charging what the market will bear	1. Income is maximised 2. Customers charged according to willingness to pay 3. Larger numbers come forward compared to single pricing policy	1. Need to evaluate client price responsiveness 2. Possibility of clients feeling discriminated against
5. Separate charges for each stage	1. May act as a stimulus for articulate and motivated clients who require less staff time 2. Clients only pay for services they use 3. Can accommodate top-up costs 4. Burden of payment spread	1. Costly to administer 2. Clients may opt out of services they need 3. May prove financially unattractive to clients 4. Different rates needed for group as opposed to individual sessions

Figure 6.2 *Summary of advantages and limitations of APL costing services*

(Adapted from and used with the kind permission of Peter Kendall, Business Studies Department, Filton Technical College, Bristol.)

internal customers as well. Since the success of the APL service – and any other learner-centred service – is so dependent on effective team work, managers offering APL and related services need to encourage mutual respect, interdependence and effective communication among all staff.

The placement of the APL service within an organisation can have a significant impact on the type of management that is possible. As is stated throughout this book, APL needs to be integrated with other learning and assessment services or opportunities. It cannot be placed peripherally within an organisation, otherwise both staff and candidates may feel like 'second-class citizens'. Management and staff alike should perceive that APL is but *one* option that will help facilitate the progression of individuals. It is by no means the *only* means of assisting learners and for that reason works most effectively in the context of a range of other services and programmes.

Selected Questions

1. Are managers within the organisation committed to team building and some of the notions of TQM?
2. Does the structure of the organisation enable everyone to see their role as equal to, if different from, those of their colleagues?
3. Is the APL service appropriately linked to other programmes and services within the organisation?
4. Do advisors, assessors, and support staff regularly meet with one another and the APL manager?
5. Does the APL manager foster regular and on-going communication with others in the centre?

Monitoring and evaluating the APL service

Monitoring and evaluating the APL service are critical activities that should be conducted on a regular basis. Because the success of APL is so dependent on maintaining the clarity and effectiveness of each stage in the process, the quality of the monitoring and evaluation will require the involvement of everyone connected with the service: advisors, assessors, support staff, managers and of course the candidates themselves.

Monitoring involves checking the on-going quality of the service. 'Formative evaluation' is another way of describing the monitoring process. Is the service, for example, meeting the standards and expectations of those who make use of it and those who contribute to it? To effectively monitor an APL service, the providing centre needs

- to identify what regular, on-going information needs to be collected, and
- to set performance indicators so that the information collected can be judged against these indicators.

Monitoring and evaluation require the collection, analysis and interpretation of information to determine whether the service or programme is meeting its overall objectives. In the context of APL, monitoring and evaluating are most often geared to *improving* the service for subsequent candidates, the staff who provide the service and the organisation itself.

Designing the evaluation

There are several different types of evaluation: quantitative, qualitative and goal-free.

- Quantitative is based on the collection of precise information, for example, the number of people completing the assessment process or the number of credits awarded.
- Qualitative is based on the views and opinions of people involved in the process, for example, the feedback candidates might provide about the advisory services.
- Goal-free evaluation involves an unstructured approach which assumes no pre-conditions of information. A discussion or interview about the need for the service

would be an example of a goal-free evaluation (Irving, 1989).

In designing the evaluation, staff of the APL centre will want to use some combination of these to collect the information they need. But first, of course, they need to know what it is they want to evaluate! Many centres begin their evaluation design by posing questions for each APL stage. For example, at the pre-entry stage they may want to ask:

- What is the demand for the service?
- What are the most effective methods of promoting the service?
- What are the motivating forces of clients seeking the service?
- What are the demographic characteristics of the candidates? (Irving, 1989)

Although each centre will be different, for each stage staff will want to ask a range of other questions, for example:

Profiling

Are the self-assessment materials user-friendly?
How much time do advisors spend with the candidates?
How long does it take candidates to complete the process?

Gathering evidence

Are the portfolio development workshops cost-effective?
Do candidates from a particular field require special support?

Assessment and accreditation

How long does it take an assessor to review a portfolio and complete the assessment?
What types of evidence do candidates present?
How many units were requested, assessed and accredited?

Post-assessment guidance

What type of new learning do candidates request?
Have candidates been satisfied with the service they have received?

Once the questions have been posed, centre staff will need to determine the best sources for collecting the information they need. Some possibilities include:

People	*Methods*
Candidates	Application forms
Advisors	Questionnaires
Assessors	Letters
Employers	Discussions
Centre managers	Interviews
Verifiers	
Support staff	

A number of points can serve to ease the actual data collection (Irving, 1989):

1. *Utilise existing systems whenever possible.*
Information that occurs normally as part of the on-going service can often yield information for both monitoring and evaluation. For example, application forms, minutes of meetings, workshop evaluation forms can all provide valuable quantitative and qualitative information.

2. *Consider the ease of collection.*
It is important not to impose extra work on staff or candidates. To do so may prevent them from completing other work, and there is also a high risk that they will not provide the information requested.

3. *Minute all APL team meetings.*
This can provide not only a rich source of information but also

149

offer a historical perspective as the service develops. Often staff are surprised at how much they have accomplished in a relatively short time.

4. *Collect reasonable samples before the analysis begins.*
Centres need to make sure enough candidates have completed the process before they begin the evaluation. Collecting information too soon or using a sample that is too small will not provide a realistic or accurate evaluation.

5. *Establish clear questions to be answered.*
The key to sound evaluation, just as in assessing candidates, is to ask the right questions. Only then can the centre determine the best methods of collecting the sought-after information.

Linking implementation to monitoring and evaluation

In more successful APL centres, monitoring and evaluation are intrinsic aspects of the implementation process itself. As we have seen earlier, this principle is found in Total Quality Management (TQM) systems. When information is collected, analysed and interpreted on an on-going basis, the centre is

- never 'shocked' by the outcomes of an evaluation;
- better prepared to deal with problems or issues while they are still manageable; and
- more able to make logical and cost-effective modifications to the service.

Summary

Implementing APL requires careful consideration of the organisational purpose and the strengths and structure of the organisation. Because APL is based on a number of assumptions not always found in traditional educational and training organisations, an institutional audit needs to investigate the readiness and willingness of the staff to deliver the APL service. Ideally the audit should look at the centre's mission, its premises, its written and visual information, the skills and training needs of the staff, the availability of flexible learning options, the nature of the learners making use of the service, the framework by which learners progress through the system, costs and fees, and the management structure.

The outcomes of the audit may reveal points of tension between the needs of individuals and the administrative or resourcing needs of the organisation. The outcomes will also permit the centre to map out an action plan for overcoming obstacles, drawing on the strengths of the staff and designing an appropriate training programme by which staff will be able to offer the APL service.

Monitoring and evaluating should be linked to the actual implementation of the APL service. By monitoring and evaluating the service on an on-going basis, the organisation will be well placed to address critical issues and improve the overall service and the effectiveness of the staff.

Chapter 7

Implications for Staff Development

Accreditation of prior learning offers significant challenges and opportunities for those responsible for staff development. As we have seen throughout this book there are a number of different development issues that may need to be addressed before the staff is competent to deliver the APL service. They may require development in technical areas such as assessment and non-directive advising and in non-technical, but equally important areas, such as communication and effective team working. In this chapter we will describe principles of best practice in delivering APL staff development, provide guidance on basic topics that need to be addressed and review expected outcomes of an effective training programme.

Principles of good practice

The first principle of good practice in APL training was described in the last chapter: the need for the organisational audit. Clearly, training staff cannot develop a sound development programme without knowing the skills, knowledge and abilities of the staff within the centre. Similarly they cannot develop the programme without knowledge of the organisation's current or likely policies. And lastly, they cannot proceed without the commitment from the management of the centre of adequate resources to do the job.

152

These three requirements are equal partners in forming the basis of a sound APL service as shown in Figure 7.1.

Figure 7.1 *The organisational requirements of a sound APL service*

If any one is lacking, there will be a high level of frustration among those who are trying to implement the service and an inherent weakness in the system.

Characteristics of an effective training programme

A training programme for APL needs to be experientially based. Because there is so much 'doing' in APL, many of the processes are best understood by experiencing them first hand. The programme also needs to be highly interactive so staff members learn to work together and, as in all training, the purpose, objectives and expected learning outcomes must be clearly articulated and agreed among all the training participants.

Experientially based
Because APL is delivered and supported by adults, it is essential that the training programme be built on the principles of 'andragogy' rather than those of 'pedagogy'. As described by Michalak and Yager (1979) pedagogy is characterised by a belief that:

- there is always a 'right' answer;
- rote memory is a good way to facilitate learning;
- the need for learning should be dictated by the instructor or teacher;
- the teacher should decide the content;
- students or trainees lack relevant experience and knowledge;
- the teacher or instructor is the source of wisdom; and
- the teacher or instructor evaluates the trainees.

By contrast andragogy is viewed as a learning process in which both the trainee and instructor (or facilitator) assume joint responsibility for the content, timing, process and people to whom the training is offered. Andragogy is characterised by a belief that:

- the trainee should accept the content of the programme based on evidence of need, not blind faith;
- trainees should be active rather than passive;
- all trainees have experience in the subject and therefore bring something with them to the training event;
- the trainee has individual needs that must be addressed;
- discussion and experimentation are sound ways of fostering learning; and
- the trainee should evaluate him or herself.

During APL training events, it is essential for the trainers to build on the notions of andragogy. They need to engage the participants in some aspects of the planning and/or the delivery of the training programme; they need to draw on the expertise of the group to develop the examples, activities and discussion points used in the training event. There should be ample time for individual reflection and small group discussions and various opportunities should be made available for the participants to evaluate their own progress and the overall training programme.

The primary job of the trainer is to *facilitate* the development of each individual learner *and* the group. The sound delivery of

APL is dependent on the strengths of each member of the APL team and their ability to work effectively as a group. To no small degree APL generates a strong synergistic effect – that is, working together the group is capable of a far greater result than might be expected of single individuals. In planning APL development, this is a critical point for training staff to remember.

Having said that the APL trainers are there to facilitate the development of the group and its individual members does not mean that the trainers can undertake the training without having a sound knowledge and some experience of key APL areas such as assessment, advising and effective management. Although the group will do much problem-solving on its own, the trainer must provide accurate and clearly defined input to serve as an appropriate stimulus for the group. The trainer should also have an adequate knowledge of the concepts with relevant examples to draw on in order to respond to the workshop participants' questions and concerns.

A range of techniques

Experienced and effective trainers try to use a range of techniques in their training programmes to promote experiential learning. As well as providing an interesting diversity for the participants, good trainers recognise that people learn in different ways. Some people may find role plays, for example, an exciting way of trying out new concepts and behaviours. Others may be more comfortable working with written case studies followed by small group discussions. So, including a range of techniques in the training programme is not just of cosmetic value: diversity can provide an essential ingredient in helping individual participants to learn in the most effective ways they can.

There are many different techniques that can be used during an APL training event. These include:

- case studies;
- demonstrations;

155

- role plays;
- simulations;
- games;
- observation;
- small group discussions;
- small group inquiry; and
- activity-based projects.

With all of these, however, the trainer must prepare well in advance and be clear about the *reasons* for introducing each activity. It is also important to add that for most sessions in an APL training event, the trainer will need to provide some input to introduce the subject and provide a focus for the group work. As far as possible, the trainers should try to involve participants even during these input sessions. A number of effective strategies can be used. For example, as part of the input session, the trainer can ask the participants to define concepts, give their opinions about or describe some aspect of the content that would be of common interest to the group.

Good facilitation is central to an effective training event. APL is no exception. Improperly facilitated activities can undermine the most cleverly designed training programme. A knowledgeable trainer who is also a competent facilitator is an essential ingredient to ensuring an effective APL training programme.

The more interesting and relevant the participants find the training event, the more likely it is that they will retain what they learn and grow in self-confidence to deliver one or more aspects of the service.

Clear learning outcomes

As with any good training programme, the trainers – and ideally, a small group of the people to be trained – need to set clear objectives for each portion of the training as well as for the overall training programme. These objectives, or expected learning outcomes as they are sometimes called, need to reflect behavioural outcomes whenever possible. A behavioural outcome suggests what the trainee will be able to *do* as opposed to simply *know* at the conclusion of the session. Consider the following:

At the conclusion of this training programme, participants will be able to:

- conduct an APL portfolio development workshop;
- apply sound principles of assessment to a range of candidate evidence; and
- develop a range of APL support materials for candidates.

These statements clearly describe expected behaviour outcomes and serve as critical points of evaluation for both the participants and the trainers. Each individual at the end of the training will be able to assess whether or not he or she has achieved what they had hoped or planned to accomplish. So too can the trainer assess the effectiveness of the training strategies used to facilitate each person's progression. If most people feel they achieve the outcome, then most likely the training programme will be considered successful.

It is worth noting that many training programmes do not specify expected learning outcomes in this way. Rather they either provide information about the *content input* or they offer non-behavioural objectives which may be difficult for both learner and trainer to assess. Consider the following examples:

In the training programme, the following topics will be covered:

- APL advice;
- APL assessment; and
- support materials for APL candidates.

Although this sort of approach gives participants a rough idea of the areas to be addressed, without expected learning outcomes, participants have no way of knowing whether the training programme will be relevant to their needs. For example, the topic of APL advice could be handled in any number of ways: at one end, it could simply provide information about the process;

at the other extreme, it could offer an intensive experientially-based learning opportunity for advisors already very experienced in APL support and guidance. Also, input statements alone provide no framework by which either the learner or the trainer can evaluate whether or not the desired outcomes (whatever they were!) were met.

Similar problems arise when non-behavioral objectives are set. Consider this example:

At the conclusion of this training programme, the participants will . . .

- appreciate the characteristics of a portfolio development workshop;
- understand the principles of assessment; and
- know about APL support materials.

Again, in and of themselves, there may be nothing wrong with statements such as these. However, how can 'appreciate', 'understand' or 'know' be assessed outside the context of doing?

Would it be sensible for the trainer to develop paper and pencil tests when the whole point of APL training events is to help people become competent to deliver the various functions of the service? Equally important, how will the participants themselves know that they 'appreciate', 'understand' and 'know' unless they can apply what they know to the needs of a range of candidates and within an organisational context?

Well-written expected learning outcomes serve to inform the participants about the content and the level of the training session and also provide adequate standards by which they can measure their own development. It must be added, by the way, that if candidates can successfully conduct a portfolio development workshop, they can also be judged to 'appreciate' the characteristics of a portfolio development workshop. Similarly if they can appropriately apply principles of assessment to a range of candidate evidence, it can also be judged that they 'understand' these principles, and so forth. No additional knowledge or understanding assessments are needed.

Costs, time and facilities

Clearly costs, time and the nature of the training facilities are also important to the design of an effective APL training programme. As most professional trainers know, almost anything is possible – given enough time, money and staff!

However, in the case of APL, the training should be geared to meet the needs, both initial and on-going, of the people who are going to be involved in contributing to the delivery of the service. Ideally, these needs will have been identified during the organisational audit and the management will have committed sufficient resources – money, people and facilities – to allow the training staff to develop the training programme needed. However, most organisations operate in less than an ideal way, so the training staff must often make difficult decisions regarding the best use of the money, time and facilities available.

Training staff often have important partners in this decision-making process who are frequently overlooked: the participants themselves. If the participants can be part of the overall planning strategy for the training event, they can contribute not only ideas and suggestions prior to the event but will come to the event with a clear understanding of imposed constraints and limitations.

Developing the basic APL training sessions

There are several sessions around which almost all APL training events are organised. There are others which may be included, depending on the context in which APL is being offered and the prior experience of the workshop participants. In this section, key sessions are outlined and some possible learning outcomes suggested. Clearly, the staff responsible for the training will want to modify or adapt these to suit the needs of the likely participants.

At the outset it is assumed that the training event is being designed to enable people to *deliver* APL. Although this event may be preceded with a briefing session to give people an idea of what either APL or the training will be about, the sessions that follow are designed to prepare people to actually deliver the full range of services needed.

Normally, an APL training event works best if there are no more than 25 participants. This is large enough to encourage diversity and interaction and small enough to ensure that each person can get what he or she needs from the event. Generally speaking, the training should include a good mix of those people who are to provide advice, assessment and management functions. Some centres also find it is useful to include marketing, public relations and administrative staff, especially those who have responsibility for recording the outcomes of the assessment process. Each centre, or groups of centres, will need to identify their own APL teams.

Experience suggests that it is best if the *entire* team undergoes the same training event, and that everyone covers all modules. Even though people serve different functions within the APL process, it is critical to their effective work as a team and to the success of the programme for each not only to understand the other person's functions but to develop a sense of what it is like to *actually* provide that function. The more knowledgeable and skilled each member of the team is, the more likely it is that together they will be able to provide a coherent and learner-centred service. Returning to the basic TQM notion as well, if each member of the team is aware of the responsibilities and needs of his or her fellow team members, each will be able to respond more quickly and sensitively to others' requests.

One further word about who should be included in the training event. If support staff are not included in the primary sessions, it will be necessary to organise a second training event to meet their needs. Support staff, whether receptionists, secretaries, administrators, telephone operators, security guards or others, play a critical role in the delivery of APL. Since candidates regularly telephone, come in for appointments, request information, complete forms, etc, support staff need to be knowledgeable about the process, the needs of candidates, the advisors and the assessors, the resources required, fees charged and so forth. And beyond that, they need to understand as well as the staff who are actually delivering the service, why APL is important to the centre, how it fits in with other offerings, and how it relates to the mission of the organisation. All too often support staff are ignored when APL is first introduced, much to the detriment of the APL team and of course of the candidates themselves. An organisation sincerely committed to 'putting the customer first' will always fully develop support staff. They should be viewed as equal members of the APL team. (It is worth noting that more than one APL candidate has reported getting as much support from the advisor's secretary as from the advisor him or herself!)

The basic training sessions

Within any given context, the exact number and length of sessions will vary considerably. However, suggested *minimum* times are provided to give the reader a rough idea of what may be required. These times assume that the workshop participants have some theoretical ideas about APL and the candidates they are likely to work with, but no actual experience. Clearly, each of these sessions could be expanded (or contracted), depending on the needs of the group, the training time and resources available and the experience and professional judgement of the trainer. In addition, the actual training event could happen over varying lengths of time.

Introduction: 30 minutes
This session will allow the workshop participants and the trainer to introduce themselves. It should also allow the trainer to welcome the participants, to outline the training format and schedule and begin to create a friendly and effective learning environment. By the end of this session the participants should be able to:

- identify the trainer and other participants by name; and
- identify the purpose and framework of the event.

Adult learners: who they are and what they want: 1 hour

The purpose of this session is to introduce the basic idea behind APL and begin to show its relevance and benefits to all learners, even those in the room! Since many people coming to APL training events often think that the service is only for those *not* in the room, it is often useful for the trainer to create or describe a theoretical situation that would require the participants to use an APL service and then ask them to identify aspects of their own past learning. It is also useful in this session to ask participants how they would prove to others that they really know and can do what they claim. By the end of the session, participants should be able to:

- describe the basic purpose of APL;
- give examples of how they are themselves adult learners and possible APL candidates; and
- begin to raise issues about evidence and assessment.

Beginning the APL process: 2 hours

This session will introduce participants to the basic APL model. It should give them an opportunity to distinguish between the role of the advisor and the role of the assessor. It should also allow them to identify and question some of the basic principles and features of APL, eg, assessment not linked to any particular training or learning programme. At the end of this session the participants should be able to:

- describe the basic APL model;
- identify the key roles and responsibilities of advisors and assessors; and
- apply the basic principles and features of APL to a range of case studies or exemplars.

Providing advice to individuals: 3 to 5 hours
The purpose of this session is to give candidates an opportunity to explore one of the major roles of the APL advisor, that of providing advice and support to candidates. The session should allow the participants to develop the staged interview and use it with one another. By the end of this session, the participants should be able to:

- listen more effectively;
- use a range of techniques to encourage the candidate's reflection on past experiences;
- use a range of support materials, eg, checklists or learning outcome statements; and
- conduct an APL interview, using a staged approach.

Developing the portfolio: 2 hours
This session should be designed to introduce participants to the concept of the portfolio and to give them an opportunity to identify examples of possible evidence. If possible, examples of strong and weak portfolios should be available for analysis and discussion. By the end of this session, the participants should be able to:

- describe the characteristics of a strong portfolio;
- identify possible sources of evidence; and
- begin to match evidence to standards or learning outcomes.

Principles of assessment: 4 hours
Although the participants will already have begun to raise a number of issues related to assessment, this session should focus on specific technical issues, eg, validity, sufficiency, currency, etc. It should also allow participants to distinguish between direct and indirect evidence and encourage them to apply a range of assessment techniques to either role play or case study situations. By the end of the session, the participants should be able to:

- define and apply principles of assessment;
- distinguish between direct and indirect evidence; and
- apply a range of techniques to role play or case study situations.

Reviewing the portfolio: 2 hours
This session should give participants hands-on experience of reviewing and recording the outcomes of portfolio segments. It should also allow them to address issues of consistency (reliability) and raise issues that they will want to deal with after they have processed a few portfolios of actual candidates. By the end of this session participants should be able to:

- systematically review a portfolio;
- record the outcomes of that review;
- develop a hypothetical assessment plan; and
- raise pertinent issues.

Giving feedback to candidates: 1½ hours
This session should be constructed to maximise the participants' opportunities to improve their overall communications skills, particularly their ability to listen and give constructive feedback. Both advisors and assessors need to be good communicators. This session should allow the participants to identify their strengths and development needs. At the end of this session participants should be able to:

- listen more effectively;
- respond to a range of hypothetical candidate needs;
- identify ways of giving feedback constructively and sensitively; and
- identify their own development needs in this area.

Developing the portfolio development workshop: 3 hours
In many respects this session can serve to synthesise key points from all the previous sessions, because in developing the portfolio development workshop, participants must be able to

facilitate the progression of the candidates in much the same way as they have been doing throughout the APL training event. This session should allow participants to develop a programme for delivering the portfolio development workshop and have an opportunity to identify various ways certain segments might be delivered. At the end of the session the participants should be able to:

- refine a draft programme for delivering a portfolio development workshop; and
- deliver the workshop to a range of candidates.

Developing support materials for candidates and the team:
2 hours
This session should allow participants to identify the support materials they will need for candidates and themselves. These may include such items as an application form, marketing leaflets, a guide to portfolio production, recording forms for assessors, feedback forms for candidates to complete at the end of the process and so forth. At the end of this session participants should be able to:

- identify the support materials needed by candidates and the APL team; and
- produce draft outlines for some of the materials.

Managing APL: 3–5 hours
This session should cover a wide range of topics, including setting fees, marketing and promoting the service, creating administrative services and processes and so forth. Every centre will have different requirements, so it is important that the training event provides enough information to allow participants to begin to determine the needs of their own centre. By the end of this session participants should be able to:

- identify their own management and administrative needs;
- develop a draft marketing plan; and

- develop a draft proposal for setting fees.

Developing a team and personal action plan: 3–5 hours
This session should allow the APL team to develop an action
plan for implementing the APL service and each member to
describe what he or she is going to do. For obvious reasons this
is a critical session for which adequate time – and feedback from
the trainer – must be allowed. At the end of this session
participants should be able to:

- identify key action points and time frames for
  implementing the APL service;
- identify their own roles and responsibilities; and
- plan for further development.

Training sessions adapted from this basic framework will enable
a centre to implement an effective APL service. The exact
content and times may vary but assuming that the training event
is experientially based and the participants are committed to
implementing the service, the centre should have little difficulty
in taking the APL work forward.

Expected outcomes of the training

By the end of the formal training period, the participants should
be able to move back into their centres to implement the service.
As has been suggested, however, the APL team will need to meet
regularly, match their progress to their agreed plans, and
continue to revise and modify their implementation plans. In
many respects, the most compelling and effective training occurs
when the team begins working with actual candidates. It is only
then that plans, progression routes and the quality of the advice,
support and feedback can be realistically evaluated.

Optional sessions

To some readers the suggested training programme may seem
like a heavy burden. Yet in many contexts this represents the

minimum number of sessions needed and a variety of other optional sessions may also be required. The list below provides examples of these:

- Technical areas
    Setting standards or learning outcomes
    Ensuring quality through consistency and verification

- APL
    Supporting candidates
    Monitoring and evaluating the service
    Developing a range of briefing sessions
    Marketing the service to particular candidate groups

- Organisational
    Team building
    Organisational change
    Forming new partnerships
    Total Quality Management
    Modularising the curriculum

- Personal
    Listening skills
    Presentation skills
    Leadership
    Effective management

In addition to the main training event and any optional sessions, there are a number of other ways in which to continue staff development. Every team meeting is an opportunity for team members to learn from one another and explore issues; every new candidate provides an opportunity for the staff to face new issues and resolve problems; and every exchange between team members or those outside the team provides an opportunity to share perspectives and information.

APL training is an ongoing activity. Because it is a service dedicated to the development of individuals, there is always something new to learn!

Summary

Staff development is essential to the successful implementation of APL. To be effective, the training should reflect the needs of the staff to be trained and must include organisational policies and an adequate commitment of resources by senior managers. The training programme should be based on principles of andragogy, rather than pedagogy and as such needs to be experientially based.

A range of training techniques can be used during an APL training event, for example case studies, role plays, simulations etc. Trainers or facilitators, however, must clearly identify the reason(s) for using one or more of these techniques and link them to the expected learning outcomes. The learning outcomes themselves should describe behaviour outcomes which can be used as critical points of evaluation for both the participants and the trainers.

The basic APL training sessions should include a range of sessions geared to the needs of the participants. Whenever possible all members of the APL team need to participate in the training event; if support staff are not included in the primary sessions, additional training sessions need to be developed.

Chapter 8

Lessons Learned

Although this entire book has drawn on the experiences of many hundreds of people implementing APL in different countries, this last chapter offers a distillation of key lessons learned in recent years. It is hoped that these will serve as a summary checklist for those readers who are either implementing APL or are about to. Readers already offering an APL service may also find the list useful to compare with their own experiences.

Planning the service*

● Be realistic! Set clear objectives and develop a work plan that is achievable. Many APL services begin as small development projects. These too must be well thought out and managed. Whether centres are planning a pilot project or a full service, the work plan must be clear and agreed by all members of the team.

● Better to do a little well than a lot less well. Often it is preferable for centres to offer a limited service at the start to establish all the administrative and processing details. On the other hand, centres committed to fostering a total learner-centred environment may want to train all staff, develop their

---

* Many of the ideas presented in this chapter have been drawn from Cook (1991), Plummer (1991) and Simosko (1991).

policies in keeping with their (new) mission statements, and offer APL across their entire educational and training provision.

● Make sure clear assessable standards are in place. Whether they are called occupational standards as in NVQs or learning outcomes as in many higher education contexts, all APL centres need to have standards available for both candidates and the staff to use. Centres wanting to implement APL will need to develop standards if they are not already available.

● Be prepared to modify 'accepted' APL models and draw on the experiences of others. Most centres who successfully implement APL are usually pleased to share what they have learned. Reinventing the APL wheel can be a costly and slow process!

● Involve senior management in the planning. As was pointed out in Chapter 7, adequate resources are critical to the successful implementation of APL. It is therefore essential that senior managers are *actively* involved in the planning of the service and are committed to fostering its development.

● Target client groups. In planning the service, it is important to know who the likely candidates will be. This is not just a marketing issue; it relates very much to the organisation's mission statement.

Staff development

● Identify committed people who have a strong sense of responsibility. It is worth noting that most APL managers report that involving the 'right' people in the APL service is as important – if not more so in some circumstances – than the allocation of other resources.

● Provide briefing and staff development opportunities for all staff, from senior managers to receptionists. To ensure success, plan staff development activities, heighten awareness and provide opportunities to practise.

● Set and agree clear and realistic development objectives for all staff members who are to be involved in the service. Draw on concepts from Total Quality Management to make sure that the objectives include those that spell out how different team members will support one another as well as the candidates. For example, assessors will need to provide support on a regular basis to the advisors.

● Clarify roles. Make sure that advisors and assessors know their functions and stick to them!

● Evaluate the staff development needs of each member of the team. As a result of an organisational audit or through some other mechanism, make sure that the staff development activities take account of team members' previous experience – or the lack of it. For example, many assessors will not have had experience in using standards or drawing on a variety of evidence as part of their assessments. Or alternatively, many advisors may have a lot of experience in working with adults in other contexts and would, therefore, be able to contribute directly to the staff development activities.

● Set up networks to support staff and keep them in touch during the start-up phases of the work. This is especially important to establish a coherence in the team and ensure its ability to work effectively.

● Implement staff development opportunities once the service is up and running. These opportunities should include refresher training for staff who may not have been as involved as they would have liked; training for experienced people to tackle particular issues in more depth; and, of course, training for any new people who are to be involved in the future.

● Develop a strong APL team. Hold regular meetings with all staff to air problems, address issues and share successes.

Advising and supporting candidates

● Be patient with candidates. Not all candidates will be fully able to grasp the ideas behind APL at first. They may 'feel' that there is something worth exploring but be unsure as to whether or not or how to proceed. Many candidates will need more time than might be anticipated to reflect on the significance of APL, and the work required, before becoming fully committed.

● Create realistic expectations. Although it is important for candidates to realise that APL is not an easy option, it is equally important that they do not see the process as a series of insurmountable hurdles. Advisors have a responsibility to help candidates develop a realistic idea of the APL service – what it can and cannot do.

● Be familiar with the standards or learning outcomes. It is just as important for advisors to be familiar with the standards or learning outcomes as the assessors. Although advisors will not be expected to have the technical knowledge of each area, they should have a general idea of both the level and the types of experiences candidates might have that would be relevant to particular sets of standards or learning outcomes. (They will need support and guidance from the assessors to do this well.)

● Give candidates honest feedback. If a candidate has no relevant experience or background in a particular area, the advisor needs to point that out when it is not self-evident to the candidate. Similarly, some candidates vastly undervalue their relevant experiences and accomplishments. The advisor as mentor should help each candidate develop a clear and accurate profile, giving appropriate feedback as consistently and sensitively as possible.

● Draw on a range of candidate experiences. There is a great tendency in some disciplines to encourage candidates to bring forward evidence from the workplace only. It is also important for advisors to try to stimulate candidate's thinking to include all their unpaid activities, from the home to volunteer work to uncertificated courses.

• Encourage peer-support groups. Especially when candidates are developing their portfolios, peer-support groups can provide an important extension to portfolio development workshops. Adults often prefer working together and can be of great assistance to one another. Peer support often helps to reduce the number of questions candidates bring to their advisors.

• Make sure guidelines for the construction of the portfolio are clear. Candidates often have so much material to put in their portfolios that organising it can be difficult. Advisors need to make sure that the written and oral guidelines are clear and consistent. Advisors should also plan to check each portfolio for completeness before sending it on for assessment.

• Communicate regularly with other advisors and assessors. Only through regular and open communication with other members of the team can advisors improve their skills and provide better support to candidates.

• Help candidates develop their own learning or training plans at the end of the APL process. Advisors, like assessors, need to remember that APL is essentially about developing individuals, helping them reach their own targets. Although APL may be an essential component of a candidate's overall development plan, there may be others that the centre can facilitate as well. The advisor may be able to provide information, support and guidance in these areas too.

Assessment

• Develop standards and learning outcomes. The subject specialists within an organisation need to assume responsibility for this, although as was pointed out in Chapter 7, the staff development unit may need to organise the training to facilitate the standards development work.

- Develop checklists as appropriate. For some groups of candidates it may be easier to use checklists to review their strengths rather than the standards or learning outcomes themselves (which are not always presented in the most user-friendly fashion). In these cases, the assessors will need to use the standards or learning outcomes to prepare checklists which relate more directly to candidates' actual experience.

- Provide guidance about evidence. Initially many candidates may be tempted to provide an excess of evidence. Every effort should be made by the centre, and in particular the assessors, to provide guidelines which will help candidates develop the *minimum* amount of evidence needed. Quality, not quantity, should be the message.

- Avoid over-assessing. Many assessors new to APL over-assess candidates; that is, they ask candidates to generate evidence using a number of different techniques, eg, portfolio evidence, demonstration and oral questioning. Although it may be necessary to assess some aspects of a candidate's competence or strengths in one or more ways, assessors need to focus again on the *minimum* amount of information they need to be sure the candidate has reached the standard. Over-assessing creates unnecessary work for both the assessor and the candidate and it costs money!

- Consider all types of evidence. Many new assessors are surprised by the range of quality evidence candidates bring forward. Assessors need to keep an open mind about the evidence candidates *could* bring forward and judge it by the same criteria applied to the more expected types of evidence.

- Meet with other assessors and the advisors on a regular basis. As for the advisors, the best way for assessors to develop and address key issues is to work with their colleagues!

Marketing the service

● Avoid jargon. Find ways of describing APL which have greater meaning for potential candidates. This suggestion applies to other information and services that may be connected with the APL service too. Since many candidates will have been away from formal education or training for a long time, they may be unfamiliar with many of the concepts and words professional educators and trainers take for granted. Clear, easy to read language will help them understand what is on offer by the centre.

● Raise awareness. Target specific client groups and emphasise the relevance and the benefits of the APL service to them. This may require developing more than one set of leaflets, for example, to describe the service. As appropriate, special attention should be given to the needs of disadvantaged groups and/or those with special needs.

● Put APL in context. Although APL may need to be marketed as a separate service in the beginning, whenever possible it should be linked to other programmes and services. The *idea* behind APL should be reflected in the organisation's mission statement.

● Publicise the successes of APL. Success breeds success. Capitalise on the positive outcomes of the APL service and use those to spread the word.

● Use a variety of marketing approaches. Experience has shown that one is seldom enough. It is best to draw attention to the benefits of the service in as many ways as is possible.

Costs and fees

● Build cost-effective practices into the APL service. For example, working with groups of candidates, developing user-friendly self-assessment materials, forming partnerships with others outside the organisation, may all serve to reduce costs.

• Expect the time staff spend with candidates to be reduced with experience. Advisors and assessors are often surprised at how much less time their jobs take per candidate once they have experience. Not only do experienced advisors and assessors know more about the APL process and the candidates they work with, they also have greater self-confidence in their decisions. This in turn seems to reduce the time they need to spend on each phase of the APL process.

• Try not to cut corners to reduce costs. In the long run it will be better, and more cost effective, if the centre develops a comprehensive, learner-centred service, even if that means modifying the way things were done prior to the implementation of APL. For example, it is essential that staff are available to candidates at convenient times, eg, after 5 pm. Disappointed candidates don't come back.

• Introduce a fee structure that is clear and easy to understand. Regardless of the type of fee structure a centre introduces, candidates should be able to understand what they are paying for. Charging candidates for separate services, eg, advice, portfolio development workshop(s) and assessment may be one way to ensure this clarity. And please note: charges for assessment must be related to units *assessed*, not to units credited! (The same level of work is involved in assessing a particular unit, whether or not the candidate receives credit for it. Additionally a centre that charges for units credited could be accused of having an ulterior motive in making sure candidates succeed.)

Organisational change

• Integrate APL into existing provision. APL should always be seen as just *one* option by which candidates can progress. Within any given educational, training or employment context, there will be many others. Candidates need to see how APL fits in with these other opportunities.

• Develop more flexible learning and assessment options. Because APL often challenges many assumptions and practices found in traditional education and training, centres frequently find themselves needing to develop greater flexibility in a range of other areas. The development of these options needs to be included in any long-range planning the organisation undertakes.

• Consider the learners' needs. As part of the organisational audit or other mechanism, take a fresh look at the environment, the delivery structures and systems, staffing levels and time-tables, administrative services, opening hours and information services. The nature and quality of each of these could have a significant impact on the development and implementation of the APL service.

• Encourage ownership of the APL service. Encourage people throughout the centre to learn about the service, ask questions and contribute ideas. Be sure to recognise the achievements of each individual contributing to the service – even just a thank you can go a long way to keeping people committed to doing their best!

Forming links

• Build on existing links. In today's world, most organisations already work with a range of other organisations and partners. These might include companies, unions, associations, professional bodies, libraries, colleges and universities, government agencies, training providers, consultants, etc. Many of these existing links will be useful to organisations implementing APL. Not only can they serve as potential sources of candidates, they might also be willing to commit valuable resources to the development of the service.

● Establish new links. Sometimes APL providers find it necessary to develop new links to deliver APL effectively. For example, if the centre is a traditional educational provider, the staff might find it beneficial to work with one or more employers to identify large pools of candidates. Similarly, if the APL provider is an employer, its staff might find that a local college is able to provide open or distance learning options or short 'top-up' courses for its employees.

● Offer APL as a 'skills audit' service. Because APL operates against clear, assessable standards, it can be used in conjunction with standards of occupational competence. In the UK, NVQs (or SVQs) can form the basis of this service, but in other contexts, local employer-developed standards might be used in similar ways.

Employers as APL providers

● Introduce APL to motivate staff to meet future needs. Most of this book has focused on implementing APL within traditional educational and training sectors. Increasingly, however, employers are developing their own in-house APL programmes. They are linking it to annual appraisals, training needs analysis and personal development programmes.

● Identify likely benefits to the organisation. Based on the experience of other employers, there is a broad range of benefits to be considered by employers. APL can:

- integrate personal development with organisational needs;
- foster better use of training resources;
- reward employees for their accomplishments;
- promote the upgrading of skills; and
- create a more flexible and self-confident workforce.

Quality assurance

● Develop a quality assurance system. In many contexts, APL will be a new idea. It will therefore be important for the providing centre to demonstrate on an on-going basis that it is not offering a 'cheap' or 'easy' route to credit or qualifications. Establishing a quality assurance system *within* the organisation may be just as important as establishing one that includes external verifiers.

● Identify the relevant external organisations early on in the planning. Depending on the level and context in which the APL service is to be offered, a number of different agencies may be involved in the quality assurance or verification process. If possible, they should participate in any planning or staff development events and should be notified as soon as the service is operational.

● Keep records carefully. An important aspect of any quality assurance system is having information available to those who will monitor and/or evaluate the service. Centres will want to develop and provide information about the training of their staff, the methods by which candidates were assessed and the outcomes of all assessments. For each of these, centres will need to develop recording forms and efficient storage and retrieval systems.

● Monitor the outcomes of assessments. As part of quality assurance, it will be important for the centre to monitor the outcomes of each assessment, to keep a record of the units assessed and accredited, and to retain complete information on the nature of each assessment for each candidate.

● Set up consistency checks. The work of each individual assessor should be monitored to make sure that standards are being interpreted similarly and that evidence is being used consistently. A centre may want to have more than one assessor review and assess a small sample of portfolios periodically to see

179

if the independent judgements made by each assessor are comparable.

● Monitor the progression of candidates. Candidates' success offers the most valuable quality assurance data of all. It is therefore essential that centres monitor candidates' progression after they complete their APL work. A range of questions might be asked: How well do APL candidates do in more advanced training or learning situations? Are they able to qualify for promotions in their jobs? Are they able to enter the job market for the first time? Can they be admitted to programmes offering professional qualifications? Each centre will need to identify the key questions to ask about its candidates and, as a matter of course, introduce these early on during implementation.

Summary

There is much to be learned from the experience of others who have successfully implemented APL. Although not all the ideas presented in this chapter will be relevant to all readers of this book, it is hoped that they will serve to highlight and synthesise many of the ideas presented in earlier chapters. It is hoped too that these 'lessons learned' will provide challenging examples of how APL can be integrated into organisations and the communities they serve to the benefit of staff and candidates alike.

References

Astin, A W, Anouje, C J and Korn, W S (1986) *Evaluation of the CAEL Student Potential Program*, Council for Adult and Experiential Learning, Chicago.

CAEL (1975) *CAEL Working Paper No. 6 – A Guide for Assessing Prior Experience through Portfolios*, Cooperative Assessment of Experiential Learning, Educational Testing Service, USA.

Care Sector Consortium (1990) *Draft Occupational Standards: Pilot Edition*, Care Sector Consortium.

CBI (1989) *Towards a Skills Revolution: Report of the Vocational Education and Training Taskforce*, Confederation of British Industry, London.

Cook, C (1991) APL – What Have we Learnt? Practical Lessons from Recent Development Projects in the UK, unpublished paper produced for the Employment Department, Sheffield.

Cross, K P (1981) *Adults as Learners: Increasing Participation and Facilitating Learning*, Jossey-Bass, San Francisco.

Cross, K P (1986) *Adults as Learners*, Jossey-Bass, San Francisco.

De Board, R (1989) *Counselling Skills*, Wildwood House Ltd, Hampshire.

DE (1986) *Working Together – Education and Training*, Department of Employment White Paper, Cmnd 9823, HMSO, London.

Dewey, J (1938) *Experience and Education*, Collier, New York.

Docking, R A (1990a) *Assessment in the Workplace: Facts and Fallacies*, Department of Productivity and Labour Relations, Western Australia.

Docking, R A (1990b) An A–Z of Assessment Myths and Assessment in the Workplace, paper presented at the TAFE National Center for Research and Development Conference, Assessment and Standards in Vocational Education and Training, Adelaide.

ED (1990) *Accreditation of Prior Learning: A Training Agency Perspective*, Employment Department, Sheffield.

ED (1991) *A Guide to the TECs Advertising Campaign*, Employment Department, Sheffield.

Gamson, Z F (1989) *Higher Education and the Real World*, Longwood, Wolfeboro, New Hampshire.

Gould, R (1978) *Transformations: Growth and Change in Adult Life*, Simon & Schuster, New York.

Hall, J (1991) *APL for Experienced Managers: Final Report*, MCI, London.

HMSO (1981) *A Training Initiative: a Programme for Action*, HMSO, London.

Irving, G (1989) Developing a Systematic Approach to APL, unpublished thesis, Northern College of Education.

Kanter, R M (1985) *The Change Masters*, Unwin Paperbacks, London.

Kendall, P (1990) Costing and Pricing APL, unpublished training material, Filton Technical College.

Knowles, M S (1970) *The Modern Practice of Adult Education: Andragogy versus Pedagogy*, Association Press, New York.

Kolb, D A (1976) *Learning Styles Inventory: Technical Manual*, McBer and Company, Boston.

Levinson, D, Darrow, C N, Klein, E G, Levinson, M H and McKee, B (1978) *The Seasons of a Man's Life*, Knopf, New York.

MCI (1991) *Management Standards: Implementation Pack*, Management Charter Initiative, London.

Michalak, D F and Yager, E G (1979) *Making the Training Process Work*, Harper and Row, New York.

Michelson, E and Mandell, A (1988) *Approaches to Portfolio Development Workshops*, CAEL, Chicago.

Mitchell, L and Johnson, C (1987) Selecting Suitable Methods of Assessment (working paper prepared for MSC/NCVQ Technical Advisory Group, Sheffield), in Simosko, S (1988) *Assessing Learning: A CAEL Handbook for Faculty*, CAEL, Chicago.

OU (1990) *APL: An Open Learning Pack for Advisors and Assessors*, Open University, Milton Keynes.

Plummer, R (1991) *A Guide for Advisors*, Management Charter Initiative, London.

Simosko S (1988) *Assessing Learning: A CAEL Handbook for Faculty*, CAEL, Chicago.

Simosko, S (1990) *Final Report: Identifying, Assessing and Recording the*

Personal Competences of Young People, Employment Department, Sheffield.

Simosko, S (1991) *A Guide for Assessors*, Management Charter Initiative, London.

Stewart, J (1990) Assessor's Notes, unpublished paper, Sheffield.

Tjok-a-Tam, S (1991) *The Forgotten Manager*, Management Charter Initiative, London.

Warren, J R and Breen, P W (1976) *The Educational Value of Portfolio and Learning Contract Development*, CAEL, Chicago.

Index